DEREK JETER
BORN TO BE A
YANKEE

DEREK JETER

BORN TO BE A YANKEE

• BY THE WRITERS AND PHOTOGRAPHERS OF •
THE NEW YORK POST

EDITED BY R.D. ROSEN

HARPER

NEW YORK • LONDON • TORONTO • SYDNEY

DEREK JETER. Copyright © 2014 by NYP Holdings Inc. All rights reserved. Printed in the United States of America. No part of this book may be used or reproduced in any manner whatsoever without written permission except in the case of brief quotations embodied in critical articles and reviews. For information, address HarperCollins Publishers, 195 Broadway, New York, NY 10007.

HarperCollins books may be purchased for educational, business, or sales promotional use. For information, please e-mail the Special Markets Department at SPsales@harpercollins.com.

Originally published as individual articles in slightly different forms by the *New York Post*, except for the epilogue, which was written expressly for this book.

All photographs by *New York Post* photographer Charles Wenzelberg unless otherwise noted on page 98, with the exception of the Cooperstown photos, which are public domain.

FIRST EDITION

Designed by Renato Stanisic

Library of Congress Cataloging-in-Publication Data has been applied for.

ISBN 978-0-06-236847-8

14 15 16 17 18   ov/QGT   10 9 8 7 6 5 4 3 2 1

CONTENTS

INTRODUCTION:
THIS KID IS GOING TO BE GOOD
DON MATTINGLY

Don Mattingly's playing career intersected briefly with Derek Jeter's when Mattingly concluded his four-year tenure as the Yankees' previous captain. After, like Jeter, playing his entire career with the Yankees, he was a hitting and bench coach with the Yankees before becoming the manager of the Los Angeles Dodgers.

The numbers don't lie. When you talk in terms of hits, the number of hits, Jetes is the guy. He's so special. He put himself right there with all the greats, guys like Joe D., the Mick, and Babe. He's kind of done all those things. He's a great person. He's won. He's won individual stuff, but he's won championships. I just think he has done everything you could ask from a guy that you signed as a kid.

He's a great story. Jetes is a testament to consistency and character and the way he's been brought up. Look at his mom and dad; they did a great job with him. And to accomplish what he has in New York is something special. If you love playing, New York is a great place to play because they stay on you. They are not going to let you rest on your laurels. If you struggle, you're going to get it, which pushes you to be better.

The thing about Jetes is that he is such a

fast learner. That was one thing I saw in him right away. I had the opportunity, which was really a blessing, to see him right after he signed after high school in 1992.

The next year, they bring him to camp. I see him that first year and I look at him and see this sprawl of a kid and say, it's a long way away from the big leagues. Then I see him the next year and it was a pretty good jump. And then the year after that I see him and say, we're getting there. He's almost there.

When he came up to the big leagues in 1995, I was playing first and he was playing short a little bit and I noticed every play was bang-bang. Every play he made, whether it was a routine play or a tough ball, it was a banger. I had to get out there and get to every ball as if the runner were going to beat it. I don't know if he remembers or not, but I said something to him about guys like Alan

Trammell, those guys catch it and throw it at the same time. They have their feet lined up as they catch the ball. And you know what, I watched him the next day fielding grounders and he had it. He made the adjustment. He was getting his feet in position and was throwing as he got it and I loved it. I was like, this kid is going to be good. That showed me so much about him. His learning process, making that kind of adjustment, is really what it's all about. He gets ready to play and

ABOVE: The Yankees' previous captain congratulates the latest one in 2003.

to me that's why he's been so good in the postseason all these years, because you don't see a change in him between a playoff game and the third game of the season. He's always taken the same approach. He's hit the same way. He's stayed with his strengths. He's a good lesson for guys.

All of this is why I say Derek Jeter is the greatest Yankee ever. ◆

THE KID FROM KALAMAZOO

BY BRIAN COSTELLO

JULY 11, 2011

The letters and packages arrived more frequently in 2001 when Mikael Mohamed first moved into the house at 2415 Cumberland Street, but a few still show up from time to time. When he gets his mail, every once in a while, among the usual bills and junk mail, there is a baseball or a card and an accompanying plea for an autograph. Not much of a baseball fan, Mohamed did not realize what owning Derek Jeter's childhood home might mean.

This is the blue, split-level home in Kalamazoo where Jeter's journey to baseball immortality took off. It began in West Milford, N.J., in games of catch with his grandmother, who loved the Yankees, but Jeter was molded here on this quiet Midwestern street. The arm that would eventually rocket throws to first base first threw balls off the side of the house until one of his parents came out to play with him. The swing was developed with thousands of practice cuts on a hitting contraption set up in the one-car garage.

The endless confidence was developed in a house where the word "can't" was banned, where his and his sister Shalee's achievements

OPPOSITE: Jeter in the early 1990s at Hyames Field at Western Michigan University.

were hung on the family room's Wall of Fame. In his bedroom, a full Yankees uniform hung on the wall, signifying the dream.

Now, as Mikael Mohamed discovers each time he goes to the mailbox, to many Jeter fans this is still a holy place.

. . . .

Derek Sanderson Jeter was born on June 26, 1974, at Chilton Memorial Hospital in Pequannock, N.J. When he was four, his family moved from West Milford to Kalamazoo, a city of 75,000, so that his father Charles could pursue his doctorate at Western Michigan University.

The family first lived in the Mount Royal Townhouse Complex near the college, where there was a grassy play area across from unit No. 1183, where the family lived. In his book,

The Life You Imagine, Jeter writes of endlessly playing games on that hill with his friend Doug Biro. Jeter was out there so much that the other kids began calling it "Derek Jeter's Hill."

When he was 10, Jeter moved into the house on Cumberland Street. The house had a large backyard, but the best feature in young Jeter's eyes was its proximity to Kalamazoo Central High School. Only a five-foot, chain-link fence stood between Jeter and the school's practice football field and baseball diamond, where the entire family would take turns hitting and fielding.

In fourth grade, when the teacher asked her students what they wanted to be when they grew up, Jeter replied, "Shortstop for the New York Yankees."

The family's practice routine continued through high school. Don Zomer, who coached Jeter as a senior at Kalamazoo Central, remembers seeing them after Jeter's team practices. "We'd be out here until we couldn't stand it anymore," said Zomer, sitting in the bleachers at the high school field. "Then we'd all go home and eat. I'd come back for a meeting and, sure enough, out on the field was Derek and his sister and his mother and his dad just getting a little bit more—a few more groundballs. Derek's work ethic was unbelievable. That's the thing I remember the most."

Charles Jeter coached his son in the Westwood Little League, whose complex was about a mile from the Jeter home. The competition level was raised for Jeter the summer after his freshman year when he played on an under-16 team called Brundage Roofing. The coach was a 21-year-old named Courtney Jasiak, who was intent on giving the kids "the coaching I never got." That meant pushups at home plate and over-the-top practices.

Jeter's cannon arm immediately impressed the young coach.

"You never see a kid that long and lean throwing a ball that hard," Jasiak said. "He was really quiet. He didn't say a word. He just went about his business."

Jasiak would move Jeter back and forth between shortstop and third base. It bothered Jeter, but he kept his mouth shut. Jasiak entered the team in a men's city league, where the kids faced men as much as ten years older. They got crushed most of the time, but Jeter left a lasting impression.

As the Perrigo Pirates, the league's defending champions, prepared to play the Brundage Roofing team, player-manager David Ferry saw their young third baseman warming up. "He was just coming up and throwing bullet after bullet to the first baseman just chest high. I walked in front of our dugout, which was a pretty rowdy group. I said, 'Hey guys, look at this kid at third base.' Our dugout just got quiet.

"At no time did we realize we were watching the future captain of the Yankees," Ferry said. Now, those same players try to get copies of their games' scorecards to prove they once played against Jeter.

. . . .

Kalamazoo is about halfway between Detroit and Chicago, which means there are a lot of Tigers and Cubs fans. Today, it's easy to find Yankees logos in the area, but in the late '80s

THE JETER PRINCIPLE

ON PLAYING HOOKY

Did you ever play hooky in school?

JETER: Never. I went to school on Senior Skip Day.

That's pathetic.

JETER: Isn't it?

and early '90s the only place you were sure to find the interlocking NY Yankees logo in Southwestern Michigan was around Derek Jeter's neck. He wore a gold Yankees medallion everywhere, and told everyone that he would someday be the shortstop for the Yankees. It's what he told his parents when he was about 8. In fourth grade, when the teacher asked her students what they wanted to be when they grew up, Jeter replied, "Shortstop for the New York Yankees."

"He would say, 'I'm going to play for the Yankees' and you'd say, 'yeah, right,'" said Mike Hinga, who coached Jeter for three summers with the Kalamazoo Maroons, an elite traveling team. "It wasn't cocky. He just really believed that was what he was going to do."

His love of the Yankees came from his grandmother, Dorothy Connors, who listened to the Joe DiMaggio–era Yankees on the radio and was among the mourners who walked past Babe Ruth's casket at Yankee Stadium in 1948. Jeter went to his first Yankees game with his grandmother during one of the summers he spent in New Jersey. Back in Kalamazoo, a poster of Dave Winfield hung on his bedroom wall.

In his eighth-grade yearbook at St. Augustine's, the students had to write about a fictitious 10-year reunion. Jeter wrote, "Derek Jeter, a professional ballplayer for the Yankees, is coming around. You've seen him in grocery stores, on the Wheaties boxes, of course." As a junior in high school, Jeter designed a coat of arms in his British Literature class that had a Yankee at bat in half of it and Jeter playing basketball in the other half.

When Jeter played on the Kalamazoo Blues AAU basketball team, his roommate on trips was Monter Glasper. Every night when the lights went out, Jeter would tell him how he would someday be the shortstop in The Bronx.

"I used to think it was odd," Glasper said. "I used to tease him and a few other guys would tease him. He used to sleep in New York Yankees boxers and a Yankees T-shirt."

. . . .

The doubters had good reason when Jeter was a young player. At first glance, he did not have the look of a future All-Star, standing 6-foot-2 and weighing just 150 pounds. "He was almost like a colt—long arms, long legs, very thin. You wouldn't look at that and go, 'Yeah, for sure,'" Hinga, his summer league coach, said. "But you could see there was this huge, huge upside."

Charles and Dorothy made Derek sign a contract before he entered high school, detailing rules on everything from curfew to how to treat girls.

Jeter made Hinga's Maroons as a 15-year-old in 1990, one of the youngest players ever to make the team. He played three years for the team and by the end scouts would line the fences at his games.

"He was just super nice, where so many baseball players at young ages, if they're good, they're insufferable and their parents are insufferable," Hinga said.

At this age, Jeter was sometimes too good. During one game in the Connie Mack Regional Tournament, he hit two home runs to bring the Maroons back, but the other team won when it scored a run on a Jeter throwing "error"—it was on the money, but too hard for the first baseman to handle.

The power of Jeter's throwing arm was a problem at Kalamazoo Central, too. During his senior year, coach Zomer had to move his third baseman to first base because he was the only player who could handle Jeter's throws, which were clocked at 90 miles per hour. Once, when Zomer saw the player catching the ball oddly in his webbing, he asked the kid what was up.

"He showed me his hand and it was completely black and blue from catching Derek's throws," Zomer said.

Jeter almost never made it to Kalamazoo Central, where his No. 13 is now retired in a trophy case. His parents wanted him to go to the smaller Catholic school in town, Hackett. They made a deal with him that if he made the Blues AAU basketball team, he could go to Central. The team was filled with players that would go on to Division I basketball careers, but Jeter made the team by impressing coach Walter Hall with his work ethic.

"Derek was an outstanding athlete," Hall said. "Basically, the thing that set him apart was not his basketball ability, but his athleticism and his ability to work hard. He always tried to be better than everyone else in drills. He wasn't a natural basketball player, but he was an athlete."

A lack of natural talent didn't deter Jeter, a shooting guard, from a love affair with the 3-point shot. "There wasn't a shot Derek wouldn't shoot," said Greg Williams, an assistant with the Blues, "and he could shoot it."

He loved taking the last shot for the Blues AAU team, where he faced future Michigan stars Jalen Rose and Chris Webber, and then for the Central Giant Maroons. As a senior at Central, Jeter was second in the conference in scoring. Some people thought if he went to the University of Michigan to play baseball, he might just walk on to the basketball team, too.

. . . .

Charles Jeter worked as a substance abuse counselor at Adventist Hospital in nearby Battle Creek. Exposed to the pitfalls of adolescence every day, he, along with Dorothy, made Derek sign a contract before he entered high school, detailing rules on everything from curfew to how to treat girls. Most of the people you talk to in Kalamazoo said the Jeter

you see now is the Jeter they knew then—respectful and humble.

"He was never, ever, ever cocky," said Sally Padley, who taught his British Literature class junior year. She said Jeter never sought special treatment. "You wouldn't have had any idea that he had so much talent from the way he acted."

Jeter had a few close friends like Biro, Shanti Lal and Josh Ewbanks. Long before he was dating starlets, he dated Marisa Novara for four years, beginning in his junior year.

"They were just a really wonderful couple," Padley said.

ABOVE: Jeter and Dick Groch, the scout who discovered him more than 20 years earlier.

Nonetheless, while Jeter and Maroons teammate Chad Casserly were playing catch before a game, Jeter told Casserly that someday he would date pop singer Mariah Carey, and maybe even marry her. "I just assumed he was joking around," Casserly said. "Then he ended up dating Mariah Carey. Everything he said came true."

Just months before the 1992 baseball draft, Jeter turned an ankle while trying to beat out an infield single. His coaches, teammates and even his opponents all wondered if his season was over and his future in jeopardy. But it turned out to be only a high ankle sprain and Jeter missed just a few weeks before returning. He finished the season hitting .508 and was named National Player of the Year by several outlets. The Yankees took him with the sixth pick that June and signed him a few weeks later.

THE JETER PRINCIPLE

ON HANDSHAKING

What about the time you wouldn't shake hands with the winning Little League team?

JETER: Didn't want to.

Why not?

JETER: As a kid, you don't want to shake hands with someone that just beat you.

What did your father say to you?

JETER: The message was you have to be a good sport. Win graciously and you have to lose with a little class, I guess is the best way to put it.

. . . .

The relationship between Jeter and Kalamazoo today is complex. There is tremendous pride among many of the residents in what he's accomplished and how he's conducted himself. There is also some resentment, perhaps inevitable, that he left his hometown and rarely returns. He usually comes back once a year in conjunction with his Turn 2 Foundation, which does a lot in the city. He was inducted into the Kalamazoo Central Hall of Fame in 2008 and attended the dinner.

Surprisingly, there is very little to mark that Jeter is from here. There is a display in the Kalamazoo Central trophy case with a No. 13 jersey, a plaque in the school's Hall of Fame, and a framed Yankees jersey outside the principal's office. "We don't recognize him enough," Zomer said.

There was a movement a few years ago to get the baseball field named after him, but it fizzled when the Jeters caught wind of some political pushback and told the supporters to drop it before it became controversial.

If you take a hard left at his old baseball diamond's left-field foul pole, though, you can make your way down to the blue split-level house where Jeter's journey picked up speed. Close your eyes and you can picture a wiry kid in a Yankees hat throwing balls against the house, waiting for his parents to join him. ◆

JETER'S YANKEES LEGACY BEGAN WITH A SERIES OF STUNNING BREAKS

BY JOEL SHERMAN

JUNE 1, 2012

Twenty years ago, a roar went through the Harbor View Room, a large conference room next to the kitchen at George Steinbrenner's Radisson Bay Harbor Hotel in Tampa. A group of stunned and euphoric executives rejoiced at a baseball miracle: the Red Sea of the draft had parted in just such a way that the youngster every person in the Yankees' draft war room believed must be taken was—outrageously—still there for the team's sixth first-round pick.

Kevin Elfering, the Yankees' director of minor league operations, leaned toward the speakerphone connected to the Commissioner's Office and read off an identification number: 19921292, a name, and a high school.

And with that, on June 1, 1992, Derek Jeter of Central High School in Kalamazoo, Michigan, not yet 18, was—just as he had predicted years before—a New York Yankee.

The previous year, with the first overall pick, the Yankees had taken Brien Taylor, and the negotiations had been so antagonistic en route to the lefty's record $1.55 million signing bonus that the organization decided to put out a simple statement and nothing more about selecting Jeter, so as not to provide Jeter's camp any added leverage in negotiations.

Within the Yankees cocoon, though, the elation was overflowing. Jeter was the top player on their board, grading out wonderfully as an athlete and player, and—in the team's estimation—so off the charts when it came to mental makeup that the Yankees did not care that he had been limited to 59 at-bats as a senior, thanks to that Michigan weather.

But how to explain that five teams had just bypassed Jeter, and three of them had him atop their boards? The Yanks were so dubious that Jeter would last until the sixth round that they had a scout named Joe DiCarlo parked in front of the home of a Pennsylvania schoolboy righty named Jim Pittsley, ready to begin negotiations instantly with the youngster they would take

OPPOSITE: Jeter poses with his 1994 Baseball America minor league player of the year award on the dugout steps of his future home.

1992

THE JETER PRINCIPLE

ON MISTAKES

The year you committed 56 errors in the minors and called your parents crying at two in the morning? What did your father say?

JETER: You gotta stay positive, that's the biggest thing, and you learn from your mistakes. Everybody's gonna make mistakes. I don't care how good you are, but you gotta try to turn that negative into a positive. Everyone's human, everyone's gonna face adversity—it's how you deal with adversity.

when Jeter was no longer available. (Pittsley would go on to compile a 7-12 record with a 6.02 ERA in parts of four seasons with the Royals.)

Why did those teams skip Jeter? There were hundreds of reasons, but here are a few:

1. Houston Astros owner John McMullen, who had once been a limited partner with the Yankees, had famously said, "There's nothing more limited than being a limited partner of George Steinbrenner." Yet McMullen had a lot of The Boss in him. Upon buying the team, he raised payroll and star power, notably by purchasing Nolan Ryan. But when the team went bad, he ordered a rebuild that resulted in Houston losing 97 games in 1991 and being awarded the first pick.

   That led the impetuous McMullen to suspend the rebuilding campaign. With pressure for a more immediate impact than a high schooler could make, the Astros ignored the pleading of scout Hal Newhouser, a Hall of Fame pitcher who strongly advised the drafting of Jeter. Instead, Houston took Cal State Fullerton's Phil Nevin, imagining that he would be ready when Ken Caminiti left as a free agent after the 1994 season.

2. The Cleveland Indians never wavered in their lust for Paul Shuey out of North Carolina, counting on the fire-balling righty to become their long-term closer.

3. The Montreal Expos' philosophy was to draft the highest-ceiling high school player available, having done that with their previous four first-round selections,

LEFT: Jeter smiles for several cameras at spring training, 1997. OPPOSITE PAGE TOP: The father of the unanimous 1996 American League Rookie of the Year gets a sartorial assist from his son.

which included Cliff Floyd and Rondell White. There was no doubt Jeter was the best high schooler in the draft.

However, in 1990 and '91, agent Scott Boras had forever changed the pay formula for high picks with high schoolers Todd Van Poppel and Brien Taylor, respectively. Van Poppel got a record $1.2 million, Taylor a $1.55 million deal. Montreal, already feeling a money crunch that would lead to the team's move to Washington, DC, had only $550,000 budgeted, and Derek Jeter had a University of Michigan scholarship as leverage.

The Expos took Mississippi State lefty B. J. Wallace, who never pitched above Double-A and who last year was arrested in Alabama on drug charges alleging he was making methamphetamine in his home.

4. The reps for Jeffrey Hammonds sent letters to Indians and Expos officials, warning them not to take the Stanford outfielder. They wanted a big deal from a big-market team and the Baltimore Orioles had become a big-market team two months earlier, when they opened Camden Yards.

With Cal Ripken, Baltimore felt no need for a shortstop; moreover, under team president Larry Lucchino, the team had focused on college players in the first round, including another Stanford player, Mike Mussina. So the Orioles gave Hammonds $975,000.

5. The Cincinnati Reds were the team the Yankees feared most. Of any baseball official, special assistant to the GM Gene Bennett had talked the most to the Jeter family. Bennett had already mined the Midwest to help bring Barry Larkin, Paul O'Neill, and

He's not going to Michigan," Groch told Livesey. "He's going to Cooperstown."

Chris Sabo to the Reds. He regarded Jeter as such a good athlete that he figured Jeter could play center until Larkin retired.

Bennett knew Reds scouting director Julian Mock had seen Jeter only as a senior, when his ankle was hurt, and that he preferred the power arm and bat of Central Florida's Chad Mottola. Still, when Bennett heard a Reds official say Mottola's name in the speakerphone, he thought it was a practical joke—until he heard: "The New York Yankees are up."

That was the moment when the Yankees' war room erupted in cheers. The day before the draft, Yankees scouting head Bill Livesey had asked Dick Groch if Jeter would accept that Michigan scholarship to play for former Tigers catcher Bill Freehan. Groch, the New York scout best acquainted with Jeter, and who was intoxicated by the mix of talent and temperament, told Livesey, "He's not going to Michigan. He's going to Cooperstown." ◆

I think people take him for granted. I think guys have played with him, played against him, see it. He's all about winning. And guys around the league want to be Derek Jeter, and that's just because he's the perfect example." —JORGE POSADA

THE CORE FOUR

BY JOEL SHERMAN

SEPTEMBER 9, 2013

What Buck Showalter saw first was Mariano Rivera's stat line, Andy Pettitte's waistline and Derek Jeter's bottom line. Just transitioning from minor league manager to major league coach himself in 1990, Showalter had a passion for player development and pored over organizational stats. He noticed one prospect's 58 strikeouts and seven walks in 52 innings. Sure, it was only rookie ball, but this was a prospect to watch.

"And then I heard what they would do to break up the monotony on Sunday, when they would let the pitchers hit and field, and I put the stats with the guy they told me was the best center fielder on the team," Showalter said. "That was Mariano."

After the 1992 season, Showalter, now the Yankee manager, was asked by then Yankees bullpen coach Tony Cloninger to have a heart-to-heart at the Instructional League with a pitcher who had just completed Low-A ball, whom Cloninger had taken a liking to, a left-handed pitcher he thought needed to get into better shape. So behind a protective screen in short center field in Fort Lauderdale Stadium, Showalter discussed conditioning

with Andy Pettitte by telling him, "Don't let anything get in the way of your success besides the hitters."

That same year Showalter met the Yankees' first-round draft pick, sixth overall, and what stood out—even though Jeter was still a teenager—"was that he had real alert eyes,"

OPPOSITE: Rivera, Jeter and Pettitte, three of the Core Four. RIGHT: Jeter with Posada, the fourth.

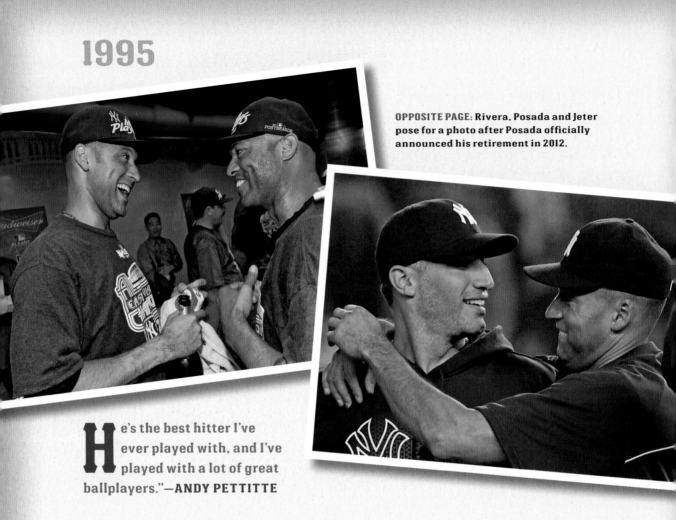

He's the best hitter I've ever played with, and I've played with a lot of great ballplayers."—ANDY PETTITTE

Showalter said. "You knew he could play point guard. Nothing would go on in his environment that he did not see. He would see all the cutters. He was sharp, aware of his environment, in control."

Three years later, in what would be his final year as Yankees manager, Showalter would guide the major league debuts of Rivera, Pettitte and Jeter.

Many years later, Pettitte could remember that in the spring of 1995 it was still a time for rookies to be seen and not heard—that Showalter didn't even make eye contact with him. With camp nearly ready to break, and the traveling secretary nagging him about whether to ship his car to Triple-A Columbus or New York, Pettitte finally worked up the nerve to walk into the manager's office and seek some guidance.

"Send your car to New York," Showalter said.

And the Four were on their way to forming the Core. Rivera and Jeter would both show up in May, bounce back and forth to Triple-A. Jorge Posada came in September. All but Jeter were on the Division Series roster. Rivera moved from starter to reliever. Posada was—of all things—mainly a pinch-runner. Showalter asked the organization to let Jeter travel with the team, knowing it would be a good learning experience for someone who would be vital in the future.

Showalter would not be part of that future. Eighteen years later, now the Baltimore Orioles' manager, he looked across the field before a Yankees game, and watched what he had helped come to pass. "You won't see anything like this happen again," Showalter said, meaning that four players could show up in one place at one time and play the highest level for

Iwould say that I was blessed. I was blessed to play with a player like Derek. Not many people have been blessed that way."—**MARIANO RIVERA**

as long as that quartet. Depending on how you feel about Johnny Damon and Jason Giambi, you could argue that the four best players to debut in 1995 were all Yankees—Jeter, Rivera, Pettitte and Posada.

If you were drawing up a blueprint for long-time contention, how could you do better than begin with a dynamic catcher, shortstop, lefty starter and closer? There are many reasons the Yankees have been great for two decades, but

nothing has been more critical than that core. That cornerstone.

"There are too many variables for that to ever happen again," Showalter said. "And what you have to remember is the makeup of those guys. The common thread was their agenda. They didn't branch off. They didn't want to disappoint each other. They were guys who never wanted to let their teammates down. You know how hard it is to make as many good decisions on and off the field as those guys made for as long as they made them, while playing in New York? They all had grips on realities at a young age in New York City.

"We just won't see that again." ◆

There are too many variables for that to ever happen again. And what you have to remember is the makeup of those guys. They didn't want to disappoint each other."

Derek takes the field.

THE GIFT OF GRAB

BY JOEL SHERMAN

APRIL 2, 1996

Omar Vizquel blooped a pitch to a place essentially that only he himself could reach in time to catch the ball. The finest shortstop in the world had hit the ball to no-man's-land in shallow left. If the ball dropped between left fielder and shortstop yesterday, as it surely would, the Indians would be within a run, with the top of their lineup due up, and Yankee starter David Cone out of the game with two outs in the seventh.

But there was someone else who could make that catch. Only a few people knew it, since this was Derek Jeter's first game in what would be his first full major league season. Jeter made an over-the-shoulder catch worthy of Jerry Rice, highlighting what was a glorious opening day for the Yankees and for the rookie shortstop in particular.

"To me that was the biggest play of the game," said Yankee coach Willie Randolph, who was Jeter's infield guru.

There was so much to like in the 7-1 Yankee rout. Cone showed no lingering effects from either his 147-pitch Game 5 playoff outing in 1995 or a shaky spring as he held the best lineup since the Big Red Machine to no runs in seven refuse-to-give-in innings.

Joe Torre outmanaged his counterpart,

Mike Hargrove, in one key top-of-the-eighth sequence and Steve Howe delivered two crucial outs in the bottom half. Paul O'Neill supplied an afternoon of clutch hits, including an RBI single off Paul Assenmacher, against whom he had been 1-for-18 with nine strikeouts. And the Yankees remained the only visiting team that can withstand the heat of Jacobs Field, where they are now 7-2.

But under crisp blue skies and in nippy 38-degree weather that made sweatshirts all but mandatory for the players, it was Jeter who was the unexpected star of stars. Who would have guessed that the best defensive shortstop in the house would be Jeter, whose fielding skills have been questioned, and not Vizquel and his magical glove?

Who would have guessed that the first

home run of the Yankees' season would be hit by a guy who had had none in his 48 at-bats the year before?

"Jeter was great," Torre said in what actually might have been an understatement.

It was an impressive start for a player with a difficult assignment—a rookie starter on George Steinbrenner's veteran team. The safety net of backup Tony Fernandez, out at least until midseason with a fractured elbow, was gone. And, across town, a defensive wizard named Rey Ordonez was already poised to be the New York favorite in any first-year comparisons.

"I know Rey pretty well," Jeter said. "We're good friends. I saw *SportsCenter* [ESPN's highlights of Ordonez's wonderful defensive showing in his Mets Monday opener], but I didn't say, 'He had a good game, so I'm going to have a good game.'"

Jeter had the good game, anyway, to say the least. It began inauspiciously, when the 21-year-old was tricked in the second inning by a man nearly twice his age. With men on first and second and two out, 40-year-old Dennis Martinez dropped down to a sidearm delivery—something Jeter did not know was in his repertoire—to fan him, looking.

But the Yankees like Jeter not just for his level swing, but his level head. He did not take the at-bat into the field. In the bottom half, he completed a seamless pivot on a double play and made a gorgeous, backhanded stop of a Sandy Alomar smash before rising to his feet to throw out the Indian catcher.

Jeter led off the fifth by socking a 2-0 Martinez fastball up and over the plate into the left-field stands to give the Yankees a 2-0 lead. It was the first opening-day homer by a Yankee rookie since Jerry Kenney in 1969 and

ABOVE: Over-the-shoulder catches like this one, and his opening day grab in 1996, became routine.

gave Jeter half as many homers as he had all last year in 138 games in the minors and 15 with the Yankees.

"It was a lucky moment," Jeter said. "I don't hit homers. I wouldn't expect too many more."

The Yankees also like that Jeter is so modest for a youngster bursting with this much talent. He would again describe as "lucky" his key seventh-inning play, but luck does not help you in no-man's-land. Only skill.

The Yanks were clinging to a 2-0 lead with Alomar at second and two away when Vizquel lofted Cone's 118th pitch to a space even speedy left fielder Gerald Williams would not get to in time. Jeter said he believed he was going to catch the ball off the bat. Cone figured differently, that Alomar would score to half the Yankee lead and that he would be yanked with leadoff hitter Kenny Lofton up next.

No wonder Cone waited for the rookie near the dugout to offer congratulations and thanks. ◆

All season the team has been the beneficiary of divine intervention— and now fan intervention as well.

JETER HAPPILY ACCEPTS ASSIST

BY STEVE SERBY

OCTOBER 10, 1996

The umpires screwed the Orioles again last night. This time the umpire was Rich Garcia and this time no one spat at him, not even Roberto Alomar. This time a 12-year-old boy with a baseball glove and a dream reached over the right-field fence at Yankee Stadium and turned a fly ball, possibly an extra-base hit, by Derek Jeter into a home run that tied the game in the eighth inning so Bernie Williams could win it with a Ruthian home run off Randy Myers three innings later.

When Yankees 5, Orioles 4 was finally over, someone asked Jeter what message he would like to send Jeff Maier, darling of New York. Jeter, just 10 years older than Maier and once one of those little boys himself watching from the seats at Yankee Stadium, smiled and said: "Attaboy!"

The Orioles had every right to scream "We wuz robbed" and curse both the umpires and the fates, and the Yankees acknowledged their good fortune. All season the team has been the beneficiary of divine intervention—and now fan intervention as well.

Someone asked David Cone, who starts Game 2 of the ALCS today, what he would

OPPOSITE PAGE: **Jeff Maier steals the ball from Baltimore—and gives Derek Jeter a home run.**

like to say to Jeff Maier. Cone smiled and said: "Come back tomorrow!"

"He'll probably be on David Letterman. He's a hero!" added Tim Raines, who was in the on-deck circle when Jeter hit an 0-1 fastball off Armando Benitez that, by all rights, should have ended up in Tony Tarasco's glove.

It is only fitting that Jeter was in the middle of all this because he has been in the middle of everything in this Rookie of the Year season. Jeter, who was born to play in New York and is destined for stardom, had four hits last night and is now 11-for-22 in the playoffs.

"He threw a fastball down the middle for a strike," Jeter said. "The second one was a fastball away. I thought I hit it too high. It kept carrying. I thought it might have a chance."

Tarasco, who had just entered the game for

Bobby Bonilla, made a mistake when he waited for the ball to drop into his glove because little Jeff Maier wasn't waiting. It was Bob Costas who pointed out that. While they told Yankee fans not to throw anything, they didn't say anything about not catching anything.

"When you're on the road especially in a situation like that," Raines said, "you might have to jump up and catch the ball. You don't know what's gonna happen."

Maybe, if Jeff Maier doesn't reach out and pull the ball into the stands, Tarasco doesn't catch the ball. Maybe Jeter winds up on second, or on third. Raines still has to drive him home with one out. Maybe he does, maybe he doesn't. This much we know: the score isn't 4-4 until he does.

Jeter didn't feel particularly sorry for the Orioles. "'Cause that didn't win the game," he said. "That tied the game. They had opportunities to score. Bernie won the game. That didn't win the game."

He is wrong about that. It won the game because the Orioles weren't going to do anything against John Wetteland in the ninth and Mariano Rivera in the 10th and 11th—because no one does anything against Wetteland and Rivera with money on the line.

"It's a judgment call," Jeter said. "Sometimes you're gonna call it right, sometimes you're gonna call it wrong." Then Jeter repeated, "I don't think that won the game for us."

Jeter initially watched the flight of the ball and didn't know it was a home run until he saw the umpire signal home run. "I saw him go like this," Jeter said, twirling his right hand in the air. "Once he did that I just ran around the bases."

Jeter returned to a dugout and a team suddenly energized and revitalized. "We just knew we were right where we wanted to be," Darryl Strawberry said. "We just knew we had to pick it up from there."

Strawberry was asked if he would have felt robbed had he been in the Oriole clubhouse. "Yeah, if you saw the replay you would feel like you were robbed," Strawberry said. "The play is not in slow motion. He can only see the play in fast motion. He made the call he thought was the best in that situation."

Cone was asked the same question. "If I'm on the other side of that call, hell yeah, I'm disappointed and I'm wondering What If," he said. "I saw the replay and it wasn't conclusive to me whether he [Tarasco] would have caught it or not. If I was in that clubhouse I'd be pretty depressed. Pretty angry."

Joe Girardi didn't see the quote unquote home run. "But I've kinda heard he wasn't gonna catch it so if he doesn't catch it we're looking at a double or a triple," Girardi said, "and then Rock gets a hit . . . but this game's a lot of judgments and everyone's doing the best they can. Every ball and strike is a judgment call. We're all gonna make mistakes out there. That's why we play the game. They don't do it by computer."

Jeter said he never saw the replay. "It really doesn't make a difference," Jeter said. "We won the game, that's the bottom line."

Someone asked Joe Torre about fan interference at Yankee Stadium and he said, "I think it happens in Camden Yards, too. To me, some calls go for you, some calls go against you. It's all part of the game."

Jeter was asked if he had ever caught a baseball at Yankee Stadium when he was 12 years old. "No, not at all," he said.

Someone wanted to know whether he would take care of little Jeff Maier sometime and Jeter smiled and said, "If I see him."

Attaboy. ◆

. . . .

Jeff Maier and Derek Jeter met a year later before a card signing in Secaucus, N.J., in 1997. Maier and his father had a brief private meeting with Jeter, who signed a ball for the 13-year-old and posed for some photographs. "He was a really nice guy," Maier said years later. "He and my father exchanged some banter. He called my father, 'Sir.'"

YANKEES' SHORTSTOP SHORT-CHANGED; JETER DESERVED MVP NOD

BY GEORGE A. KING III

NOVEMBER 19, 1998

Perhaps it was too simple for 26 of the 28 seamheads who voted for the American League's Most Valuable Player, which erroneously went to Rangers right fielder Juan Gonzalez yesterday. Had they not needed a formula such as hits plus runs plus RBIs plus homers plus walks plus stolen bases minus strikeouts, pop outs, ground outs to figure it out, then they may have been able to arrive at the proper conclusion.

Derek Jeter was the MVP of the AL.

Yet only Mike Sullivan, out of the Cleveland chapter of the Baseball Writers' Association of America by way of the *Columbus Dispatch*, and myself voted that way. Twenty-one of the writers cast first-place ballots for the very talented Gonzalez and five went for Red Sox shortstop Nomar Garciaparra.

In winning his second MVP, Gonzalez drove in a ton of runs. Garciaparra stamped himself as a superstar in the making by finishing second in his second big league season thanks to hitting many baseballs over AL walls.

However, if you paid close attention all summer, Jeter was the choice. How could the MVP of a team that set an AL record of 114 regular-season victories not be the league MVP?

"He had a defensive season that was like [Omar] Vizquel. I don't think the Yankees could have done what they did if Jeter didn't have the type of year he had," Sullivan said.

And he was hardly a slouch on offense. Yes, Gonzalez helped the Rangers win the AL West by driving in a league-leading 157 runs and clubbing 45 homers. Sure, Garciaparra lifted the Red Sox into the AL Wild Card spot by batting .323 and driving in 122 runs. But Jeter's .324 average—fifth in the league—was one point higher than Garciaparra's and six points better than Gonzalez's. Jeter led the league in runs scored with 127, compared to Garciaparra's 111. Jeter's 203 hits—third in the AL—were eight more than Garciaparra had and 10 more than Gonzalez.

How could the MVP of a team that set an AL record of 114 regular-season victories not be the league MVP?

And that just begins to tell the story of how valuable Jeter was. It says here that without Jeter's bat in the No. 2 hole, his career-high 19 homers, and 84 RBIs, his flawless defense and quiet leadership, the Yankees don't run away and hide from the Red Sox in the AL East. And if they don't do that, they wouldn't have been able to set themselves up for a dominating postseason. Don't forget for a nanosecond that the reason they spanked Gonzalez and the Rangers three straight in the AL Division Series was that the Yankees spent September fine-tuning instead of sweating a pennant race.

"He was excited about the news," Jeter's agent Casey Close said last night of his client's third-place finish in the voting while Jeter and Mariner shortstop Alex Rodriguez attended a charity event in Florida. "And a little surprised."

Think about the one player Yankee fans would hate to have seen go down for an extended period of time. Of course, it was Jeter. Bernie Williams spent five weeks on the DL and the Yankees went 21-10. Tino Martinez wasn't right for a month after the senseless drilling he received from the Orioles' Armando Benitez and the Bombers survived. Chuck Knoblauch never got it going. Scott Brosius had a wonderful bounce-back season but he made a team-high 22 errors compared to the unbelievable nine Jeter made at short.

Yes, the Yankees were 9-3 when Jeter missed 15 days with a rib cage muscle problem, but Luis Sojo, Jeter's replacement at short, hit .200 (10-for-50). Elevated from the bottom of the order to the No. 2 hole three times in Jeter's absence, Brosius went 1-for-10 (.100). So a longer Jeter absence was certain to hurt the Yankees.

My ballot had Jeter on top, Gonzalez second, and Garciaparra third. The Indians' Manny Ramirez was fourth, followed by Boston's Mo Vaughn. O'Neill was next in front of Rangers catcher Ivan Rodriguez. David Wells was eighth, Williams ninth, and Rangers pitcher Rick Helling 10th.

That's because the award is called *Most Valuable.*

And since Jeter was the MVP of the best team on the planet, he was the MVP of the AL. At least according to the four eyes that paid attention. ◆

This is a story about what you don't see. Not about March to October, but November to February. It's not about Page Six or position 6 on the scorecard. . . . This is a story about how Derek Jeter turned a frail body and undeveloped skills into a superstar package.

THE MAKING OF DEREK JETER

BY JOEL SHERMAN

MARCH 31, 1999

This is the story of a 156-pound kid. A gawky guy who had more difficulty going to his left than Newt Gingrich. A hitter with less balance than a juggler on a high wire. This also is the story of a 196-pound man. A fluid fellow whose left is all right. A hitter who these days can balance not just himself, but an entire team on his broadened shoulders.

Both stories are about Derek Jeter. We can assume that it is going to be a heckuva ending, with likely stops in the $100 million club, Monument Park, and Cooperstown. But it would be wrong-headed to believe any of this happened on its own.

"Sure he looks like the golden boy today, but he didn't spring from his parents like this," said Yankee minor league head Mark Newman. "No one has done more than him to improve. He truly works to be a great player."

This is a story about what you don't see. Not about March to October, but November to February. It's not about Page Six or position 6 on the scorecard, but five-days-a-week at the Yankee minor league complex in Tampa. This is a story about how Derek Jeter turned a frail body and unrefined skills into a superstar package.

"You know what statement bothers me?"

Jeter said. "'Overnight success.' There is no off-season anymore. People don't understand that. I'm down here in November. People may be better than you, but no one should be a better worker than you.

"I wouldn't have drafted me," he says. "I weighed 156 pounds fully dressed. The funny thing is on the basketball program in high school I was listed at 185 pounds. I figured when I got on the scale in Tampa they would just send me home."

When Jeter was drafted in June, 1992, Shawn Powell, the Yankees' strength and conditioning coach in Tampa, remembers that "he had zero muscle on his body. None. Clothes just hung off him. I called him Gilligan in the Skipper's clothes." ◆

OPPOSITE: **February 1997, in Tampa, Florida.**

You know what statement bothers me?" Jeter said. " 'Overnight success.' "

As others worked out, Jeter mockingly flexed his skin and bones in the mirror. Jeter's body was no surprise to the Yankees. Covertly, they had sent 10 different people into Kalamazoo to scout the frail-looking Jeter at Central High. "Skill-wise, though, a man among boys," said Brian Sabean, then the Yankees' VP of scouting and now the Giants GM.

"We hoped against hope he would be there at number six," said Bill Livesey, now Tampa Bay's director of personnel, then the Yankee scouting director. Somehow five teams passed on the 17-year-old voted best high school player in the nation. The Yankees pounced. The only skinny that concerned them was the informational type.

"He was really immature physically, but we knew it was just the opposite with his personality," said Newman, then the Yankees' minor league field coordinator. "He was weak physically, but you could close your eyes and see

what tomorrow would be. And you knew he would get there because of his makeup. He has gotten there by lifting weights every day of winter."

Starting in November 1994, Jeter began a five-day-a-week, off-season regimen designed by Powell. He has put on 40 pounds of muscle, increased strength dramatically across the board, and not lost quickness.

"He is now the example for all the other kids who come in to lift in the off-season," Powell said.

Jeter struck out just once in 59 at-bats as a high school senior. On his first day as a pro—July 2, 1992—in a Gulf Coast (Rookie) League doubleheader, he went 0-for-7 and whiffed five times. He remembers feeling "overmatched."

"There were times he told me 'I shouldn't have done this,' that he should have gone to college," Mark Newman recalls.

In the cool climes of Kalamazoo, the seasons were short and so were the fastballs. "Everything was in fast-forward in pro ball," Jeter said. He needed a late burst to bat merely .202 in the GCL.

"His first year he hit .202, but he could

THE JETER PRINCIPLE

ON NOT GETTING ANY SATISFACTION

If you had to give me one reason why you've been relentlessly, consistently successful, what would that reason be?

JETER: Never satisfied. You can never be satisfied with anything that you've done, because once you do that, it's time to go home.

> **I** don't think it's just his discipline on the field. I think it's his all-around discipline about who he is and what he stands for and to always have been a consistent worker and always has tried to get better." —JOE GIRARDI

ABOVE: September 1996, in Yankee Stadium.

field," says Livesey, then the team's scouting director. "The second year, he hit, but he made fifty-six errors. People started talking about him as a center fielder. That is when you have to go back to the tools. The tools and the work ethic."

"But it was obvious he had the characteristics you look for in good hitters," said Gary Denbo, Jeter's manager his first two minor league seasons. "He had bat speed, he was fearless, and he was a coach's dream from the outset. He worked hard every day."

No one in the Yankee family knows Jeter's swing like Denbo. Starting in early January, the two begin a seven-week program into spring training. The focus has been on balance and on turning on inside fastballs. This past off-season they worked on pulling the ball with greater backspin so that there is more carry. That, and added weightlifting, moved Jeter to tell Powell his goal is 24 homers this year, five more than 1998.

"We've only scratched the surface of his ability," Denbo said. "It might be strange to say that with all the success he has had, but I think he is still learning how to hit. I think he has a higher ceiling than Nomar Garciaparra and Alex Rodriguez."

In January, Jeter also begins taking grounders daily off the bat of Trey Hillman, the Columbus manager. If another player joins the drill, regardless of how long Jeter's been at it, he stays to take the last grounder.

"He is as competitive taking balls in Tampa as he is in a major league at-bat at Yankee Stadium," Hillman said.

Hillman's tutelage is augmented during the season by Yankee coaches Willie Randolph and Don Zimmer, who added great range to Jeter's left by breaking his habit of reaching for balls with two hands. The result was just nine errors last year, none in his final 40 games, including the playoffs.

"It is very impressive what he does to enhance his God-given ability when there are no reporters around and no cameras," Hillman said. "He's working. Anyone would have understood if he didn't pick up a bat or glove after either of the championship years, and if he had gone on cruise control. But the taste of a championship and personal success only made him hungrier. That is why I think he's going to get even greater."

Stay tuned. ◆

ALL THE RIGHT MOVES

BY TOM KEEGAN

OCTOBER 27, 2000

Kurt Abbott's bat shattered and the barrel made it all the way out to the infield dirt, in front of the shortstop. So what did Derek Jeter do with the barrel of the shattered bat? The right thing, of course. He waited for the batboy to sprint out to his position and he handed it to him.

That's who Jeter is. Give him a situation and he does the right thing, whether it's with a whole bat in his hands at the plate or just part of one in the infield.

Jeter, 26, held something else in his hands later—the hardware that identified him as the World Series MVP, so named after his home run tied a game the Yankees would win 4-2 with a pair of runs in the ninth inning.

Jeter became the first player ever to win the All-Star Game MVP award and World Series MVP honors in the same season. Frank Robinson is the only other player to win both awards during a *career*. Jeter became the third shortstop to be named World Series MVP, joining Bucky Dent (1978 Yankees) and Alan Trammell of the 1984 Tigers.

From the last out of Game 3 until the first pitch of Game 4, the World Series could have belonged to either the Yankees or the Mets.

ABOVE: Sixth inning, Game 6 of the Subway Series. Going, going, gone.

ABOVE: Jeter gives manager Joe Torre a celebratory shampoo after beating the Mets.

That's when Derek Jeter, leading off for the only time in the Series, unloaded on Bobby Jones, hit the first pitch of the game over the fence, and put the World Series back in the Yankees' control.

And there he was again last night, drilling another one over the fence, this one on a pitch delivered by Al Leiter to tie the game in the sixth inning.

And there he was throughout his fourth victorious World Series, making all the plays, delivering all the throws on the money.

And there he was, running the bases with seamless efficiency.

Jeter used this World Series to make himself the king of baseball in New York, the biggest Yankee since Reggie Jackson and well on his way to becoming the biggest since Mickey Mantle.

He has a hit in 14 consecutive World Series games and is a .342 career World Series hitter. He has reached base safely in 55 of 61 postseason games. In his fourth World Series, Jeter batted .409 with two doubles, one triple, and two homers. He set a five-game World Series record with 19 total bases and tied five-game records with six runs and nine hits.

Jeter used this World Series to make himself the king of base-ball in New York, the biggest Yankee since Reggie Jackson and well on his way to becoming the biggest since Mickey Mantle.

"MVP, you could have picked a name out of a hat," Jeter said. "It seems like we have a group of 25 MVPs. First game, [Jose] Vizcaino came up. What Paul O'Neill's done, our pitching staff, our bullpen, Mariano Rivera, today Luis Sojo. You don't rely on one guy. You have to get contributions from everyone."

Jeter knows better than to assume he can take going to the World Series for granted. He knows better than to bypass a chance to savor a World Championship. "You don't know when you're going to have an opportunity to get back," Jeter said.

Every World Series winning clubhouse in the television era is packed with players who stare into the camera and claim, "everyone wrote us off." As a rule, that claim is hogwash. In this instance, the claim is justified. Everyone did write off the Yankees in late September and with good reason. They lost 15 of their final 18 games and took a seven-game losing streak into a postseason that started with a Game 1 loss to Oakland.

"Every year is a different story," Jeter said. "I'd be lying if I said this one wasn't more gratifying. I mean, we struggled this year. We've had tough times. We said before, winning isn't easy. We made it look easy. It's something that's very difficult to do. We've had our bumps in the road."

None of those bumps threw the Yankees off course in winning another World Championship, their 26th. "Oakland was the hottest team in baseball when we beat them," Jeter said. "Seattle was tough. The Mets have the best team I've seen in the five years that I've been here."

This wasn't the best of the five Yankees teams for which Jeter has played, which of course, is completely irrelevant. The Yankees won the World Series, which means everyone had a great year for them, as O'Neill is fond of saying, and he's right.

The Yankees will have a different look next season, despite winning it all. But, as Jeter said, "We have to have a chance to enjoy this before we worry about what's going to happen next year."

Jeter has all winter to enjoy it and he's sure to find under his Christmas tree a contract that will ensure he remains in pinstripes for a long, long time. ◆

THE JETER METER

HOW HE MEASURED UP AT THE BEGINNING OF 2014

ALL-TIME CAREER HITS

1. Pete Rose 4,256
2. Ty Cobb 4,189
3. Hank Aaron 3,771
4. Stan Musial 3,630
5. Tris Speaker 3,514
6. Cap Anson 3,435
7. Honus Wagner 3,420
8. Carl Yastrzemski 3,419
9. Paul Molitor 3,319
10. **Derek Jeter 3,316**

ALL-TIME CAREER SINGLES

1. Pete Rose 3,215
2. Ty Cobb 3,053
3. Eddie Collins 2,643
4. Cap Anson 2,614
5. Willie Keeler 2,513
6. **Derek Jeter 2,470**
7. Honus Wagner 2,424
8. Rod Carew 2,404
9. Tris Speaker 2,383
10. Tony Gwynn 2,378

YANKEES BATTING AVERAGE

1. Babe Ruth .349
2. Lou Gehrig .340
3. Earle Combs .325
3. Joe DiMaggio .325
5. Wade Boggs .313
5. Bill Dickey .313
7. **Derek Jeter .312**
8. Bob Meusel .311
9. Robinson Cano .309
10. Don Mattingly .307

YANKEES HOME RUNS

1. Babe Ruth 659
2. Mickey Mantle 536
3. Lou Gehrig 493
4. Joe DiMaggio 361
5. Yogi Berra 358
6. Alex Rodriguez 309
7. Bernie Williams 287
8. Jorge Posada 275
9. **Derek Jeter 256**
10. Graig Nettles 250

YANKEES RBIS

1. Lou Gehrig 1,995
2. Babe Ruth 1,971
3. Joe DiMaggio 1,537
4. Mickey Mantle 1,509
5. Yogi Berra 1,430
6. **Derek Jeter 1,261**
7. Bernie Williams 1,257
8. Bill Dickey 1,209
9. Tony Lazzeri 1,154
10. Don Mattingly 1,099

YANKEES RUNS

1. Babe Ruth 1,959
2. Lou Gehrig 1,888
3. **Derek Jeter 1,876**
4. Mickey Mantle 1,677
5. Joe DiMaggio 1,390
6. Bernie Williams 1,366
7. Earle Combs 1,186
8. Yogi Berra 1,174
9. Willie Randolph 1,027
10. Don Mattingly 1,007

YANKEES HITS

1. **Derek Jeter 3,316**
2. Lou Gehrig 2,721
3. Babe Ruth 2,518
4. Mickey Mantle 2,415
5. Bernie Williams 2,336
6. Joe DiMaggio 2,214
7. Don Mattingly 2,153
8. Yogi Berra 2,148
9. Bill Dickey 1,969
10. Earle Combs 1,866

YANKEES EXTRA-BASE HITS

1. Lou Gehrig 1,190
2. Babe Ruth 1,189
3. Mickey Mantle 952
4. Joe DiMaggio 881
5. **Derek Jeter 846**
6. Bernie Williams 791
7. Yogi Berra 728
8. Don Mattingly 684
9. Jorge Posada 664
10. Bill Dickey 617

YANKEES TOTAL BASES

1. Babe Ruth 5,131
2. Lou Gehrig 5,060
3. **Derek Jeter 4,739**
4. Mickey Mantle 4,511
5. Joe DiMaggio 3,948
6. Bernie Williams 3,756
7. Yogi Berra 3,641
8. Don Mattingly 3,301
9. Bill Dickey 3,062
10. Jorge Posada 2,888

YANKEES DOUBLES

1. Lou Gehrig 534
2. **Derek Jeter 525**
3. Bernie Williams 449
4. Don Mattingly 442
5. Babe Ruth 424
6. Joe DiMaggio 389
7. Jorge Posada 379
8. Robinson Cano 375
9. Mickey Mantle 344
10. Bill Dickey 343

YANKEES GAMES PLAYED

1. **Derek Jeter 2,602**
2. Mickey Mantle 2,401
3. Lou Gehrig 2,164
4. Yogi Berra 2,116
5. Babe Ruth 2,084
6. Bernie Williams 2,076
7. Roy White 1,881
8. Jorge Posada 1,829
9. Bill Dickey 1,789
10. Don Mattingly 1,785

YANKEES STOLEN BASES

1. **Derek Jeter 348**
2. Rickey Henderson 326
3. Willie Randolph 251
4. Hal Chase 248
5. Roy White 233
6. Ben Chapman 184
6. Wid Conroy 184
8. Fritz Maisel 183
9. Brett Gardner 161
10. Mickey Mantle 153

THE JETER PRINCIPLE

ON THE WISDOM OF FATHERS

What's the best piece of advice your father gave you growing up?

JETER: Never let someone outwork you.

The best piece of baseball advice growing up?

JETER: Never make excuses.

The best piece of advice he's given you as an adult?

JETER: Enjoy the moment.

JETER PULLS OFF MIRACLE, FANS FLIP

BY TOM KEEGAN

OCTOBER 13, 2001

Leave it to Derek Jeter to come from nowhere and instinctively do the right thing to fix a broken play and a broken team. In the latest illustration of why he is a better baseball player than statistics could ever capture, Jeter blended his smarts and his athleticism—the two tools that make him a great baseball player— and turned a potential game-tying run for the other team into an out for his.

As hard as runs are to come by in a division series that just became a great deal more interesting with the Yankees' 1-0 win over the A's last night at the Coliseum, turning one run into one out is the equivalent of hitting a grand slam.

With two outs in the seventh inning, Jeremy Giambi standing on first base, and the Yanks leading by a run but down two games to none in the five-game set, Terrence Long ripped a double down the right-field line. Shane Spencer dug the ball out of the corner and rainbowed a throw well over both cutoff men, Alfonso Soriano and Tino Martinez, as A's third-base coach Ron Washington waved Giambi home. The ball seemed destined to skid into futility, enabling Giambi to easily score the tying run.

Enter Jeter. Think about it: Are you ever driving home from the Stadium, asking yourself this question: "Why in the world did Jeter do that?"

No, you're not. Never. Because he always does the right thing.

Do you ever watch a game on television and ask yourself this question: "How in the world did Jeter do that?"

Like a great point guard or a clever quarterback, Jeter sees plays that most players don't.

I respect him as much as anybody in the game. Look how he handles himself. He cares about the team. He has integrity. He's stand-up. . . . Doesn't matter if he's not hitting well. You're going to get the very best out of him. It's part of the reason I respect him so much." —TERRY FRANCONA, FORMER BOSTON RED SOX MANAGER

He tends to be in the right place at the right time.

"This game is about instincts and he has instincts," said Luis Sojo. "Anyone else just stays on the mound."

Sprinting across the infield, Jeter intercepted the ill-fated baseball about a third of the way up the base path. His momentum was carrying him into foul territory and Giambi was chugging toward home.

In about the time it takes to blink, Jeter removed the ball from his glove. Recognizing that he had only one way to get the ball to home plate in time, Jeter threw a sideways pass to Posada.

ABOVE: The Flip makes Jeremy Giambi look foolish for forgetting to slide.

"Everyone was like, 'What the [heck] was he doing there?'" said Sojo, who watched in awe from the bench. "I've never seen that play."

Oakland's on-deck hitter Ramon Hernandez motioned for Giambi to slide. He chose not to. Bad decision.

More evidence that stats don't always tell you the truth: Spencer, who made an awful throw, and Jeter, who revived a dead play with a brilliant improvisation, received equal credit, both getting assists.

Reggie Jackson wondered why anyone would be surprised that Jeter would make such a play. "Great player," Reggie said. "He's big-time. He's a big-game player. We all know that."

"He makes great plays in big situations," said Spencer, who more than anyone should be relieved that he does. "He may not put up the numbers of some other guys, but he's the best in the clutch."

Jeter explained his job on that play is to act as cutoff man for a throw to either third or home. Once he saw Washington wave Giambi home, he was able to commit to trailing the first and second cutoff men on a throw to the plate.

"It had to be one motion," Jeter said. "I didn't have time to set up, plant, and throw. I just got it on one hop and it was more of a reaction thing. It wasn't like I thought it through."

Asked if he had ever made a play like that to home plate, Jeter said he had not, but acknowledged that "you win a lot of games that way, by doing the small things. We pay attention to detail. We paid attention to detail the first two games and got beat."

The Yankees now have to pay attention to one more detail: It takes three losses to be bounced from a Division Series, not two. ◆

. . . .

The Yankees went on to win the next two games to take the Division Series from Oakland and beat Seattle in the League Championship Series before losing to Arizona in the World Series.

FORGET OCTOBER— JETER PROUD OWNER OF NEW MONTH

BY WALLACE MATTHEWS

NOVEMBER 1, 2001

You can add one more item to the array of honorifics, titles and awards Derek Jeter can expect to amass by the time his major league career is over: Mr. November. The month was brand-new when Jeter claimed it as his own, and one hopes not for the last time. In the bottom of the 10th inning last night, he hit Byung-Hyun Kim's 3-2 pitch into the lower right field seats to tie the World Series at two games apiece.

Just like that, the calendar changed and so did the World Series.

Just like that, a game in which the Yankees were one out away from being one loss away from losing the Series became a heart-stopping win.

And just like that, a player who had taken most of October off had reestablished his credentials in the first-ever baseball game played in November.

Jeter was the MVP of last year's Subway Series, but this year he was a candidate only for LVP—Least Visible Player. In 15 previous at-bats this World Series, Jeter had managed just

OPPOSITE: Jeter's 10th-inning home run wins Game 4 of the 2001 World Series.

one harmless single in the third inning of Game 3. Even his mother was getting impatient.

"She's been yelling 'Do something!' for four games," Jeter admitted.

So, like a dutiful son, he did.

And with one swing of the bat, all eyes were on Derek Jeter again, and all eyes are on the Yankees, who have improbably, but not impossibly for this team, drawn even in a Series that was running away from them.

"Surprising things happen in this game," Joe Torre said, "but after a while, things cease to surprise you, because this ballclub never quits. It's remarkable to be able to come back like that. It just shows you, you can never quit on this team."

Or, as Jeter said, "We always feel as if we have a chance to win a game," moments after his home run gave the Yankees the come-from-behind 4-3 victory. Up to that moment, the Yankees might have been the only ones to feel that way.

With two out in the bottom of the ninth, the Arizona Diamondbacks needed just one more out to push the Yankees to the brink of elimination in a World Series for the first time in four years.

The air had gone out of the sellout Yankee Stadium crowd. Even the bleacher people seemed to have run out of enthusiasm and invective.

And then Tino Martinez, the target of trade rumors for most of the season and the sole source of Yankee power for much of the second half, crushed the first pitch he saw from Kim over the center-field fence with Paul O'Neill on first to tie the game at 3.

At that point, the game was won everywhere but on the scoreboard for the Yankees, who had Mo Rivera ready to pitch the top of the 10th inning and Mo Mentum batting for them in the bottom.

Enter Jeter, who had single-handedly kept the Yankees' postseason alive with his jaw-dropping shovel pass to Jorge Posada to save

Mike Mussina's 1-0, series-turning win in Game 3 of the ALDS versus Oakland. But he cooled off steadily thereafter and, after tumbling into the photographer's box in Game 5 of the ALCS against Seattle, had practically disappeared.

Jeter took two sliders for strikes, then worked the count full. The next slider came in fat and went out fast, curling just inside the right-field foul pole.

And this 27-year-old, who, improbably, has four World Series rings to show for five big-league seasons, was so excited he leaped onto home plate with both feet. "I think I broke my foot doing it," he said.

More likely, he broke the Diamondbacks.

"Obviously, it's a huge boost for us," he said. "I mean, going down 3-1, that's a pretty deep hole for us. But this win means absolutely nothing unless we come out and play well tonight."

Yesterday, the month and the Series were just about over. But today is a new month and a new Series. And Mr. November is just getting started. ◆

. . . .

Unfortunately, Arizona repaid the Yankees with a come-from-behind, bottom-of-the-ninth victory in Game 7 to win the Series.

THE JETER PRINCIPLE

ON NOT BEING PERFECT

Ozzie Guillen called you "The perfect man." Tell me how you're not the perfect man.

JETER: How I'm not? There's a lot of reasons why I'm not, but I'm not gonna share that with you.

How about one thing you could change about yourself?

JETER: I think it takes me a long time before I trust someone. But I think that's a good trait to have.

BOSS GRANTS DEREK CURIOUS CAPTAINCY; JETER 11TH TO RECEIVE HONOR

BY GEORGE A. KING III

JUNE 4, 2003

Derek Jeter already has more money than he can spend, four World Series rings, and no trouble getting a date. Now he has one of the neatest titles in New York: Captain of the Yankees.

In an effort to shake up his stagnant but first-place club, George Steinbrenner yesterday named the soon-to-be 29-year-old shortstop the 11th captain in team history.

"It's a big day for Jeter because of the people who have been there before him," said Steinbrenner, whose team started last night's game against the Reds at Great American Ballpark 1½ games ahead of the Red Sox and two in front of the Blue Jays in the AL East.

Steinbrenner sent general partners son Hal, son-in-law Steve Swindal, and GM Brian Cashman to represent the Yankees at a press conference while he remained in Tampa and worked on the draft.

"That's a good question," Hal said when asked why his father wasn't on hand for the historic occasion.

OPPOSITE: George Steinbrenner explains baseball to one of his employees in 2000.

Jeter, whose lifestyle Steinbrenner questioned just this past December, joins an exalted fraternity that includes Babe Ruth, Lou Gehrig, Thurman Munson and Don Mattingly. Jeter is the sixth captain in Steinbrenner's 31 years and the second youngest—one month older than Munson when he was anointed on April 17, 1976.

Why now? Why wait until a third of the season was gone? Why not during this past winter? Why at all since Steinbrenner's Yankees haven't had a captain since Mattingly retired in 1995? And there was plenty of material to choose from, including Paul O'Neill and David Cone.

Why not Jason Giambi, the leader of the A's before taking $120 million of Steinbrenner's money? Why in Cincinnati and not a press conference in The Bronx with all the trimmings?

2003

Jeter, whose lifestyle Steinbrenner questioned in December, joins an exalted fraternity that includes Babe Ruth, Lou Gehrig, Thurman Munson and Don Mattingly.

"I felt a need for leadership at this point," said Steinbrenner, who believes the lack of a leader has contributed to the Yankees 12-17 record after posting a 21-6 ledger in April.

Asked if he is looking for Jeter's captaincy to ignite a spark, Steinbrenner said, "It's just one of the sparks we will have."

Jeter graciously downplayed the significance of receiving the honor away from home. "It doesn't matter, an honor is an honor regardless of where you get it. It doesn't make a difference."

Jeter won't be standing in the middle of the clubhouse, imploring his teammates to run harder in a loud voice. He is more of a one-on-one guy, and that type of leader doesn't usually ignite sparks. Yet he said he thinks yesterday's move can help the highest-paid team in the history of baseball. "I am not going to need extra motivation," Jeter said. "I am not going to change anything I do. Hopefully, we can get things going here."

In what will obviously be viewed as a jab at Torre, Steinbrenner didn't consult with the manager yesterday before telling Jeter he was the captain. Torre learned of the move from Cashman.

"Not necessarily," Torre said when asked if he thought it was odd that The Boss didn't talk it over with him. "It's his decision. It's not required for me."

Torre, who said there is no downside to the move, also didn't think Steinbrenner was taking a shot at him or his coaches. Torre said, "The coaches are an extension of me. The players know what to do. My coaches work hard, they don't just show up at game time."

Randolph, who was a co-captain with Guidry from 1986 to 1989, knew yesterday would eventually arrive, saying, "I felt one day he would be named captain." ◆

I trusted him more than any other player I had managed. I trusted him to be prepared mentally and physically every day, and to prioritize winning above all else. I trusted him to say the right thing when talking to a teammate or the media. I trusted his instincts and his calm under the greatest pressure. I trusted he would never tell me if he were hurting, even when he was, because he thought the right thing for the team was to play."—JOE TORRE

WELCOME TO THE CLUB
A LOOK AT THE FIRST 10 YANKEE CAPTAINS:

1. Hal Chase 1912
2. Roger Peckinpaugh 1914–1921
3. Babe Ruth 5/20/22–5/25/22
4. Evrett Scott 1922–1925
5. Lou Gehrig 4/21/35–6/2/41

6. Thurman Munson 4/17/76–8/2/79
7. Graig Nettles 1/29/82–3/30/84
8. Willie Randolph 3/4/86–10/2/89
9. Ron Guidry 3/4/86–7/12/89
10. Don Mattingly 2/28/91–1995

THE JETER PRINCIPLE

ON BASEBALL AND RELIGION

What do you think about when you walk under that DiMaggio quote in the runway—"I want to thank the Good Lord for making me a Yankee?"

JETER: It's exactly how I feel.

A CAPTAIN IS BORN

BY MIKE VACCARO

JUNE 4, 2003

He stops being everyone's kid brother now, the perpetually respectful young-ster who's called his manager "Mr. Torre" and his owner "Mr. Steinbrenner" from the moment he showed up for good in the spring of 1996. Hard as it is to be-lieve, Derek Jeter will turn 29 years old in another 22 days, an age when you really should be looked at less as a boy-band pin-up and more as a grown-up.

He has no choice now, of course.

Because wearing the captain's "C" for the New York Yankees is about as grown-up as sports gets. They make movies about Yankee captains. They preserve lockers for Yankee captains. It is a title for life. When Bernie Williams refers to Don Mattingly, you know what he calls him? He calls him "Captain." And Mattingly has been retired for 7½ years.

Jeter has been auditioning for the gig from his first hours as the Yankees' regular shortstop, April 2, 1996, when he hit a home run and made a spectacular run-saving, over-the-shoulder catch in the Opening Day chill of Jacobs Field. It is a role he was born to play, given his Lou Gehrig–style importance to these Yankees and his Gary Cooper leading-man looks.

The circumstances under which he assumes the title may not be ideal, and the timing is curious, and the atmosphere around the Yankees is as carnival-like as it's been in a quarter century, and it seems rather surreal that the Yankees owner could view Jeter as Captain Midnight in one breath and Captain Courageous with the next.

But the basic truth is this: Sooner or later, Jeter was going to get the job. Sooner or later, he was going to assume his rightful place in the pantheon of Yankee leaders. Sooner or later, he would be asked to take a serious leap into baseball adulthood.

Jeter has been auditioning for the gig from his first hours as the Yankees' regular shortstop.

Might as well be now.

Expect Jeter to emulate the last captain in word and in deed. On the day Don Mattingly was given his captain's bars, Feb. 28, 1991, he said, in his finest Mattingly-ese: "I'll lead by example. I'm not a talker. What's a leader, anyway? I think it's anybody who goes about his job consistently."

In their own way, those words echoed what Thurman Munson had said 15 years before, when George Steinbrenner had finally talked him into becoming the team's first captain since Gehrig. The reluctant catcher reacted to his coronation with the typically gruff observation: "Maybe they made me captain because I've been here so long. But if I'm supposed to lead by example, then I'll be a terrible captain."

Nobody much believed that, of course, in the same way that no one should be worried that Jeter's affinity for late nights and good times outside the lines will affect his leadership between them one bit. After all, nowhere in the job description does it say you need to be an ascetic to be a good captain. Or acerbic. Or anything other than what he already is.

As the Nets' Richard Jefferson said yesterday about Jason Kidd: "He has the title of captain, but even if he didn't he would be our captain, because he acts like our captain. It's who he is. It's what he is."

It's what Derek Jeter is now, and what he's always been destined to be. The kid brother isn't 21 anymore. He isn't even a kid anymore. An adult's job beckons. The time is just right, even if the timing is all wrong. ◆

RIGHT: Jeter leans on column depicting him, Thurman Munson and Lou Gehrig, who reportedly went there after hearing his diagnosis.

CAREER HIGHLIGHTS AS OF JUNE 2003

- Named 1996 AL Rookie of the Year
- 2000 All-Star MVP
- 2000 World Series MVP
- 5 All-Star Game appearances
- Ranks fifth in all-time Yankee batting average
- Most home runs by a Yankee shortstop
- Hosted *Saturday Night Live* on Dec. 1, 2001

YEAR	HR	RBI	RUNS	AVG.	SB
1995	0	7	5	.250	0
1996	10	78	104	.314	14
1997	10	70	116	.291	23
1998	19	84	127	.324	30
1999	24	102	134	.349	19
2000	15	73	119	.339	22
2001	21	74	110	.311	27
2002	18	75	124	.297	32
2003	3	12	12	.298	1
TOTALS	120	575	851	.316	168

CAPTAIN DOWN, BUT SHIP SAILS ON

BY MIKE VACCARO

JULY 2, 2004

I t had to end this way, of course, because the Yankees simply do not lose games when Derek Jeter acts as if it's October already. They do not lose when their captain dives into the stands on the dead run, when he steals two extra-inning runs away from the Red Sox, when he disappears into a crowd and emerges with his face looking like Chuck Wepner's.

When Jeter does this, it isn't a contribution, it's a duty.

The Yankees had to win. They had no choice. They had to bury the Red Sox, had to break their hearts one more time, had to send 55,265 people home with the sounds of autumn ringing in their ears. Once Jeter took off after Trot Nixon's ball with two outs in the top of the 12th inning, with two Red Sox motoring toward home plate, once he stabbed the ball, never slowed down and performed a 2½-tuck into the lower field boxes, the rest was just a matter of filling in the blanks.

The Yankees had to win. Because the Yankees always win when he does these things.

"He just has a sense, an instinct, for what he wants to do from the moment the ball is hit, and

OPPOSITE: The captain dives into the stands and comes out an even bigger part of Yankee history.

that's not something you can teach," Joe Torre said, shaking his head in wonder, marveling one more time at Jeter's off-the-charts baseball IQ. "You either can make that play or you don't. And he's made a ton of them in his day."

Jeter wasn't around to see how it all turned out, because he was in Columbia Presbyterian Hospital, having his battered body tended to by a battery of doctors. He wasn't there to watch Manny Ramirez take his super slo-mo tour of the bases after clearing the left-field fence in the top of the 13th inning, a blast that gave the Red Sox a 4-3 lead and forced even the truest mezzanine believers to think about beating the rush to the parking lot.

He was on the other side of the Harlem River by the time Ruben Sierra kept the game alive by scratching a single through the infield, and he was probably getting stitches in his chin

by the time Miguel Cairo slammed a game-tying double to the right-center-field gap.

And it didn't matter where he was when John Flaherty came off the bench to drive in the winning run on a hanging 3-1 slider a few minutes later, because as long as you were anywhere within the five boroughs of New York City, you had a good chance to hear the riotous joy spilling out of Yankee Stadium. Not that any of this would have come as even a small surprise to Jeter. He's done this before.

"Sometimes," Flaherty, the hitting hero, said of Jeter's remarkable play, "you can only shake your head and wonder at what that guy is capable of doing. It's just amazing. It really, really is."

Actually, what's amazing is just how routine all of this is, how easily Jeter has made Yankee fans expect the impossible, from the moment he made that over-the-shoulder catch in Cleveland on his very first day as the Yankees starting shortstop, Opening Day of 1996.

THE JETER PRINCIPLE

ON THE PASSAGE OF TIME

Next Saturday, is it hard for you to believe you're turning 36?

JETER: Stopped counting. It's all a mindset.

How old do you feel?

JETER: Twenty-one.

Have you asked Michael Jordan or anybody about dealing with Father Time?

JETER: Nope.

It's something you don't even think about?

JETER: No, really haven't.

Appreciate what you see with Jeter, every chance you get. You aren't likely to see his kind around here for a long, long time.

Anyone who saw his sideways flip in 2001 understands. Anyone who saw him spill into the stands a few days later understands.

There is no one like him, anywhere. Nomar Garciaparra used to be mentioned in the same sentence, sometimes in a higher paragraph, and last night we were reminded of just how foolish that really was. Garciaparra didn't play last night, in a game that just may have ejected his team from the division race,

because he was feeling "tight." You'll have to ask Garciaparra, and his conscience, how that could possibly be.

As for Jeter, you can ask him whatever you like tonight. On his way to the hospital, he told his buddy, Jorge Posada: "I'm playing tomorrow." Appreciate what you see with Jeter, every chance you get. You aren't likely to see his kind around here for a long, long time. If ever again. ◆

2,723 AND COUNTING FOR NEW HIT KING

BY GEORGE A. KING III

SEPTEMBER 12, 2009

Derek Jeter: 2,723. Lou Gehrig: 2,721. Babe Ruth: 2,518. Mickey Mantle: 2,336. Then, there's everyone else who has ever played for the Yankees. Jeter moved to the top of the storied franchise's hit list last night when he rifled a single between Orioles first baseman Luke Scott and the first-base line leading off the third inning at Yankee Stadium.

Jeter, who had struck out in the first, laced a 2-0 pitch from Orioles right-hander Chris Tillman and eked past Gehrig, a Yankees icon.

The crowd of 46,771, which was on its feet throughout the three-pitch at-bat, roared and gave Jeter a three-minute standing ovation. The Yankees poured out of the first-base dugout and each teammate, led by Alex Rodriguez, hugged the captain.

Jeter tipped his cap to the all parts of the Stadium and then pointed to a suite above the dugout, where his parents and family stood, applauding the historic moment.

"I really didn't know what to expect with the rain delay. I didn't know how many people would be there," Jeter said of the game that started 87 minutes late due to rain. "As for the team, I didn't know. I got caught off guard. It's still hard to believe for me. The whole experience has been overwhelming."

The only drawback was the Orioles hanging a 10-4 loss on the Yankees. The loss halted the Yankees' winning streak at four, shaved their AL East lead over the rained-out Red Sox to 8½ games and kept the magic number at 14.

"Now we can get back to winning games," said Jeter, who went 2-for-4, adding an RBI single to right in the fourth inning.

Hal Steinbrenner was on hand to represent his family, and before the three-minute chant of "Der-ek Jet-er, Der-ek Jet-er" was over, the Yankees had handed out a statement from George Steinbrenner.

"For those who say today's game can't produce legendary players, I have two words: Derek Jeter," The Boss said. "Game in and

game out, he just produces. As historic and significant as becoming the Yankees' all-time hit leader is, the accomplishment is all the more impressive because Derek is one of the finest young men playing today.

"That combination of character and athletic ability is something he shares with the previous record holder, Lou Gehrig. It adds to the pride that the Yankees and our fans feel today. Every Yankee era has its giants. It's thrilling to watch Derek as he becomes one of the greats of his generation, if not of all time."

Jeter, who left the game along with Rodriguez (who hit a three-run homer in the first) and Jorge Posada when rain stopped the game in the top of the seventh, spoke to The Boss.

"It was great to hear from him," Jeter said. "We have been pretty close. I miss seeing him around here. It was great to hear his voice and he had some great things to say."

With the Stadium packed and fans hanging

THE JETER PRINCIPLE

ON JINXES

By the way, your fielding percentage this year, you're at a career high.

JETER: Why would you even say something like that? Now you're trying to jinx me.

TYPE
Singles 2,005; Doubles 437; Triples 58;
Home runs 223

HIS BAT'S 10 FAVORITE BALLPARKS
Original Yankee Stadium 1,277 hits; Camden
Yards 140: SkyDome 128; Fenway Park 121;
Tropicana Field 106; Angel Stadium 91; New
Yankee Stadium 88; Jacobs Field 87; Oakland
Coliseum 86; Rangers Ballpark 80

FAVORITE OPPONENTS
Against the Orioles: 269
Blue Jays 261
Red Sox 254
Rays 239
Angels 175
Tigers 163
Rangers 159

A's 159
Mariners 156
Indians 152
Royals 137
Twins 136
White Sox 132
Mets 110

FAVORITE PITCHERS
Against Tim Wakefield 31
Sidney Ponson 29
Rodrigo Lopez 26
Pedro Martinez 22
Jamie Moyer 22
Roy Halladay 20
Aaron Sele 20
David Wells 20
Kelvim Escobar 18
Curt Schilling 18

on every movement Jeter made, the shortstop was cheered when he took his position, when he surfaced from the dugout to hit, and when a tape of Bob Sheppard announced his name.

If pitcher Chris Tillman was awed by the scene, he didn't show it when the captain stepped into the batter's box to lead off the bottom of the first. Tillman started with three 94-mph fastballs. Jeter took the first for a strike and swung through the second. At 0-2, Jeter took a ball, then fouled off a 95-mph heater. At 1-2, Tillman got Jeter to whiff with an 80-mph off-speed pitch.

History couldn't wait forever, though, and in the third inning Jeter singled his way into the Yankees' record book before adding another single in the fourth to remind everyone he was far from through. ◆

COOPERSTOWN SAVING SPACE FOR JETER

BY KEVIN KERNAN

SEPTEMBER 13, 2009

Baseball Hall of Fame president Jeff Idelson was the Yankees' public relations director when the team drafted Jeter in 1992 and conducted the first press conference for the future star. If Idelson continues at his current post for another decade, he will be there for Jeter's Hall of Fame induction speech.

"I think I will be calling him Mr. Jeter at that point," Idelson said with a smile. "You could tell how dynamic Derek was the minute we drafted him. He had a presence about him even as a high school kid. You could tell he was well-parented and well-schooled at a young age."

The hits will keep on coming. Now that Derek Jeter is the Yankees' all-time hit leader, surpassing the legendary Lou Gehrig, this is the unofficial start of the "Jeter is a Baseball God" tour.

In a much smaller way, I saw it during my years covering Tony Gwynn in San Diego. Gwynn is Padres Baseball. We all saw it with Cal Ripken in Baltimore. Ripken is Orioles Baseball.

For this generation, Yankees Baseball is Derek Jeter, and his brilliant career will reach

THE JETER PRINCIPLE

ON GETTING AHEAD OF YOURSELF

Who would you want presenting you at the Hall of Fame?

JETER: Hall of Fame, man—slow down, buddy. I don't even talk about those kinds of things.

Jeter's induction will be the Hall's Woodstock. The early estimate is that 100,000 fans will be present.

its fevered climax the day he is inducted into the Baseball Hall of Fame in Cooperstown. Figure that Jeter will play at least five more years. After the five-year waiting period, Jeter will be inducted on the first ballot around 2020.

The rolling hills of Cooperstown will be flooded with a sea of baseball fans unlike any the Hall has ever seen. The largest crowd up until now has been 82,000 for the induction of Ripken and Gwynn in 2007. Because Baltimore is within driving distance of Cooperstown, most of those fans were Ripken fans. "This is a town of 2,000 people, so we had 41 times our population here for Ripken and Gwynn," marveled Idelson.

The two other largest crowds were for the 1999 class that included Nolan Ryan, George Brett, Robin Yount and Orlando Cepeda, when 50,000 showed up, and the 1995 turnout of 40,000 fans for Mike Schmidt and Richie Ashburn, but the Hall of Fame is in New York City's backyard and Jeter's induction will be the Hall's Woodstock. A baseball happening. The early estimate is that 100,000 fans will be present to see Jeter inducted.

"When you look at the legacy of a Gehrig or a Ruth or a Mantle," said Brad Horn, senior director of communications for the Hall, "Jeter fits right in that mold."

The fact that in so many ways Jeter is now linked to Gehrig, who was inducted in 1939, makes his star shine even brighter. It's not lost on Idelson, who walks daily among the ghosts of the game. "There are a lot of similarities in their charisma, their appreciation for the game, and respect for the game and respect for the fans," Idelson said. "And, of course, their star power in New York, although neither one craved it.

"Derek has that unique ability to have the right human touch with everyone he comes in contact with, very much like Gwynn and Ripken," Idelson added. "He's a great human being."

One day not that far in the future, before a sea of baseball fans in the green hills of Cooperstown, Jeter will become, along with Gwynn, Ripken, Gehrig and the others, a member of baseball's immortal team. ◆

2011

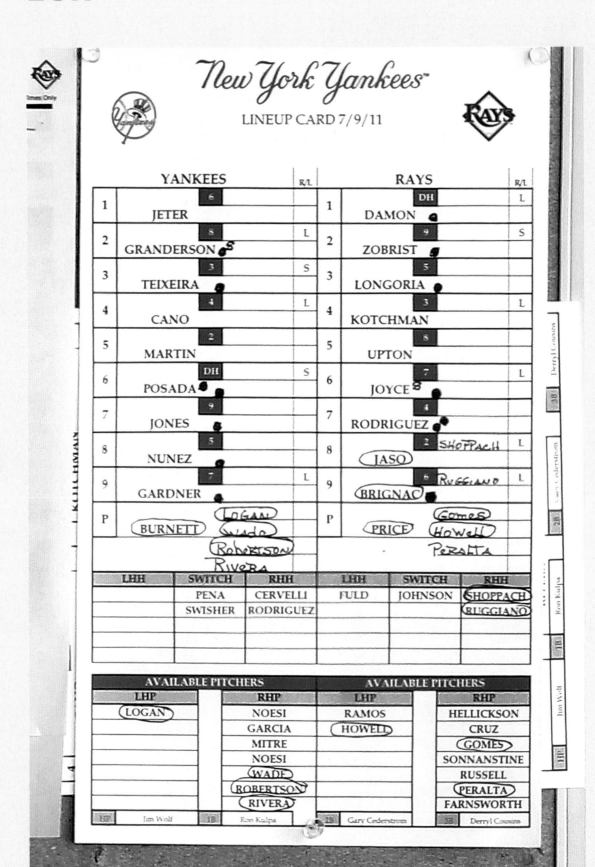

New York Yankees

LINEUP CARD 7/9/11

	YANKEES		R/L		RAYS		R/L
1	JETER	6		1	DAMON	DH	L
2	GRANDERSON	8	L	2	ZOBRIST	9	S
3	TEIXEIRA	3	S	3	LONGORIA	5	
4	CANO	4	L	4	KOTCHMAN	3	L
5	MARTIN	2		5	UPTON	8	
6	POSADA	DH	S	6	JOYCE	7	L
7	JONES	9		7	RODRIGUEZ	4	
8	NUNEZ	5		8	JASO 2 SHOPPACH		L
9	GARDNER	7	L	9	BRIGNAC 6 RUGGIANO		L
P	BURNETT LOGAN Wade Robertson Rivera			P	PRICE Gomes Howell Peralta		

LHH	SWITCH	RHH	LHH	SWITCH	RHH
	PENA	CERVELLI	FULD	JOHNSON	SHOPPACH
	SWISHER	RODRIGUEZ			RUGGIANO

AVAILABLE PITCHERS			AVAILABLE PITCHERS		
LHP		RHP	LHP		RHP
LOGAN		NOESI	RAMOS		HELLICKSON
		GARCIA	HOWELL		CRUZ
		MITRE			GOMES
		NOESI			SONNANSTINE
		WADE			RUSSELL
		ROBERTSON			PERALTA
		RIVERA			FARNSWORTH

| HP | Jim Wolf | 1B | Ron Kulpa | 2B | Gary Cederstrom | 3B | Derryl Cousins |

3,000

BY MIKE VACCARO

JULY 10, 2011

Later, Derek Jeter could laugh about a lot of things that hadn't seemed so funny at the time. He could chuckle about how the great Tony Gwynn had said that the last 10 hits leading up to 3,000 were the hardest to get. "Took me a month to get 10 hits," Gwynn said.

He could talk about how anxious he had been at the plate, how much pressure he had been under to reach the magic number on this home stand, how the usual cool façade that has served him so well for so long was little more than a carefully crafted ruse.

"I've been lying to you guys for weeks," he joshed. "I don't know if you caught on to that or not."

He even would make light of his lately acquired reputation as a slap-and-poke singles hitter, the guise he has slipped into so often during his last 1,000 or so plate appearances these past two years, when for the first time people started looking at Jeter as something other than an indestructible hitting automaton.

"I didn't want it to be a slow roller to third base," Jeter would say when asked what 3,000

OPPOSITE: **The lineup card the day the captain hit his 3,000th.**

would look like. "I didn't want to have *that* replayed forever."

Instead, he would have this: This day, fierce with sunshine and good feeling, a shared fellowship shared with 48,103 people inside a sold-out Yankee Stadium, described for millions of others by trusted voices belonging to Michael Kay, to John Sterling, or to thousands of others who simply had their ears glued to cell phones, eager to describe what they were seeing to cousins, fathers, uncles, friends who couldn't see or hear for themselves.

He would work a count against Rays lefty David Price to 3-and-2. Price, with gold coursing through his left arm, who had challenged Jeter on fastball after fastball in the first inning before surrendering 2,999; Price, of whom Jeter said: "He can throw 98 miles an hour. I wasn't looking for a breaking ball."

He got a breaking ball, 78 miles an hour.

2011

When he first came into the league, he was a young player, but he looked as if he had played the game a long time before he got here.... I admire the fact that he can control his emotions in an emotional setting.... One of the things that makes me feel good is Derek has come up to me and said, 'Thanks for paving the way.' I feel good that I might have helped change the mindset toward the bigger shortstops. ... It still blows me away that in the rich history of the Yankee franchise, nobody's had 3,000 hits and I really love that he has become the first to do it."—CAL RIPKEN

"He could've thrown it in the dugout," Jeter would say, "and I would have swung."

Fortunately, it started around Jeter's belt *and* spun slowly toward his knees. Jeter never got a chance to stride, stood flat-footed, but centered the ball perfectly.

It was exactly two o'clock in the afternoon.

And the afternoon was about to be turned upside down. The baseball soared through the air, tracing a perfect parabolic path in white against the blinding blue sky. Should we have known? Maybe we should have. We saw Jeter make that flip play all those years ago, saw him

dive into the stands a couple of times, sometimes looking like Leroy Brown afterward, with a couple of pieces gone.

We've seen him seize more moments than anyone of his generation, often with a home run. We saw him make a star of 12-year-old Jeffrey Maier. We saw him dismiss Bobby Jones and the Mets with one swing of his bat, leading off Game 4 of the 2000 World Series. Saw him hit the first-ever November World Series home run off Byung-Hyun Kim, ending a forever World Series night in that awful autumn of 2001.

RIGHT: Jeter rounds first base and heads—once again—into the history books.

"Derek," Jorge Posada would say of his friend, "always knows how to come through."

Alex Rodriguez, watching the at-bat from the bench, sitting next to CC Sabathia, had a premonition. He saw Jeter take a splendid cut fouling off a nasty Price changeup a few pitches earlier.

"CC, if he gets another pitch like that," Rodriguez said, "he's liable to hit a home run."

Then he went and he hit the home run, one that managed to leave the masses speechless and unable to stop screaming all at the same time. He clobbered a curve and sent an entire city into rapture. It shouldn't be this easy, this routine, to take ridiculously huge moments and slip into them like a Technicolor dream coat. Yet he has done just that since he was 21

CC, if he gets another pitch like that," Rodriguez said, "he's liable to hit a home run."

years old, winning an Opening Day in Cleveland with both his glove and his bat.

And rising to the occasion again on this 5-for-5 day, when, of course, he was at the plate with the winning run on third in the bottom of the eighth, and, of course, he got him in.

"That was the easy part," Jeter would say. "I've been in *those* situations my whole career."

There may even have been times when he failed to deliver in them. It was just hard to remember any on this day of days. ◆

PERFECT FIT FOR JETER

BY JOEL SHERMAN

JULY 10, 2011

This was chilling and memorable, nostalgic and surreal, impressive and historic. Yet at the end of his career, Jeter is not going to be defined by 3,000 hits. Sure, the feat is going to be on his bronze plaque in Cooperstown, this great distinction of being the only Yankee to reach that milestone.

But Jeter is going to be remembered just the way he had hoped—by winning, which is what he helped the team do yesterday by going 5-for-5, an achievement that, under the circumstances, even the humble Jeter found as implausible as a movie script.

Yesterday was meaningful beyond the obvious and momentous because the Yankees needed all that Jeter brought yesterday, at the end of a week of tough losses and injuries. The homer that made him the 28th player in history to reach 3,000 hits tied the score in the third inning, his double scored the tying run in the fifth, and his single in the eighth brought home the decisive run in the eighth in a 5-4 triumph over the Rays.

"It would have been really, really awkward to do interviews on the field and wave to the crowd if we would have lost," Jeter said.

But the Yankees won because, somehow, Jeter had this stunning performance still in him. He left even his teammates awed by his timing, the rising to the moment. Jeter had five hits between June 13 and July 8, a period that included his disabled-list stint for a strained calf. And then he equaled that number yesterday between 1:15 p.m. and 4:15 p.m., in the first five-hit game in the history of the new Yankee Stadium.

"We were all kind of, wow, he really knows how to do it," manager Joe Girardi said. "He is a big-time player in big moments."

And let's not forget that it's been a rocky road this season. On May 8 in Texas, Jeter had four hits and two homers, and the instant reaction was that, after a tough opening month and an uninspiring 2010 last year, Jeter was back. But in the next 32 games, before going on the disabled list, Jeter hit just .245 with no homers and only seven extra-base hits in 139 at-bats.

RIGHT: A bona fide immortal, and he's got the balls to prove it.

This ignited a debate over whether Jeter still belonged atop the batting order—and even if he should be playing shortstop daily. No wonder Jeter feels that the DL stint was "a blessing in disguise," allowing him to refresh his 37-year-old body, and also to work on his swing in Tampa while rehabbing. That he pulled three hits with authority yesterday was significant because hitting coach Kevin Long was trying to add more of that to Jeter's game with their off-season work together.

Jeter now has extra-base hits in four straight games for the first time since May 2009.

Yesterday, Jeter was the best player on the field, and the Yankees need more of this. Alex Rodriguez has a slight tear of the meniscus and is either going to play compromised the rest of the year—perhaps without his power—or go for surgery and be lost for about a month. Nick Swisher is struggling with a quadriceps injury. The 2011 Yankees need more brilliance from Jeter. And the winner inside him knows that perfectly well.

But at least he has put the burden of reaching 3,000 hits in the rearview mirror. It was arguably the best game of his career.

And just think for a moment about the career we are discussing. ◆

We were all kind of, wow, he really knows how to do it," manager *Joe Girardi said.*

2012

Jeter dove for the ball. And never got up.

YANKEES LOSE GAME, JETER TOO

BY MIKE VACCARO

OCTOBER 14, 2012

For a moment, it felt like nobody could breathe, nobody could move. This baseball basilica, which shook with life and with energy barely an hour before, was suddenly, sullenly silent. An hour before, thousands of them had aped the words of the great Jack Buck, watching Raul Ibanez's latest moonshot miracle.

And now they said the same thing.

Because The Captain was on the ground.

The Tigers had already retaken the lead, and while that was surprising, it isn't law that amazing comebacks are required to have satisfying endings. The Lakers lost the Jerry West Half-court Shot Game, after all. The Mets lost the Endy Chavez Game. It wasn't beyond the realm that the Yankees could lose the game.

But to lose The Captain, too?

Suddenly, impossibly, this wasn't going to be about a game lost, but something far deeper, far graver. The Tigers won the game 6-4, rendering as a footnote the Yankees' four-run comeback in the ninth, and Ibanez's fifth astonishing home run in the last three weeks. That's minor, though. That's get-'em-again-tomorrow stuff.

This was something else. Jhonny Peralta hit a ball to Derek Jeter in the top of the 12th.

Jeter dove for the ball. And never got up. He rolled on the ground, flipped the ball aside. And was in pain. Real pain. How many times have we seen him shake these things off? Ugly bruises were laughed off. Ankle sprains were dealt with.

Only once, when he'd separated his shoulder in Toronto on the opening day of the 2003 season, had Jeter ever really looked hurt, and been hurt. It had become a running joke with two different managers: Jeter grinding his way through pain, talking his way into the lineup.

There was no laughing this one off. Jeter couldn't put any weight on his leg. He was carried off the field.

Carried off the field? You'd sooner see Jeter wear a Red Sox hat onto a field than get carried off one, unless absolutely necessary.

This, clearly, was absolutely necessary.

And so this is what the Yankees must deal

LEFT: Accustomed to carrying the team, Jeter accepts a lift from trainer Steve Donohue and manager Joe Girardi.

with now: a Jeter who has a broken ankle, and a 0-1 deficit to the Tigers in the ALCS, and a star player, Robinson Cano, now 0-for-his-last-22, and a falling idol, Alex Rodriguez, who for the fourth straight game was either pinch-hit for or kept on the bench entirely.

It seemed like it was going to be such a magic night. Where were you when it happened again? Were you on the Deegan? The Bridge? Or were you one of the 25,000 or so who actually stayed to the end, who saw Raul Ibanez do it again, who saw the Yankees do it again, who knew enough that this is starting to be an October when 27 outs means 27 outs?

We know better now, all of us, those of us in the press boxes who'd already filed stories that nobody but snickering copy editors will ever read, those of you in the stands who'd hustled out to the parking lot, those of you watching on TV who opted for the opening monologue of *Saturday Night Live*.

THE JETER PRINCIPLE

ON THE END OF THE WORLD AND ITALIAN FOOD

If you knew the world would end in 24 hours, what would you do?

JETER: Spend it with family.

And what would be your last meal?

JETER: Chicken parmigiana and ice cream. Gold Medal Ribbon. Baskin-Robbins.

Fool me once, shame on you.

Fool me twice, shame on me.

Fool me again and again and again and again and again?

It was almost too good to be true. And then turned out to be precisely that. A night earlier, we'd all seen the Cardinals rise from the dead, shake off all those pitches that could have ended their season in Washington. We saw how baseball can be singularly cruel and uplifting at the same time, how it can devastate one fan base while enthralling another.

Those Cardinals were facing the end of their season if they'd lost and so the stakes were certainly higher for them. But the Yankees looked so completely hopeless and hapless for eight innings last night, stranding the bases loaded on three different occasions. They didn't seem like they could buy a big hit with Donald Trump's wallet.

Then they did. They were bulletproof. Surely they couldn't lose.

And then they did lose. A ballgame.

And then something far worse. ◆

SOME OF JETER'S FAVORITE FANS. CLOCKWISE FROM TOP LEFT: **Jordana Brewster, Anna Kournikova, Minka Kelly and Vanessa Minnillo.**

JETER'S PRIVATE HIT PARADE

Herewith some members of the all-star team of romantic partners Derek Jeter has fielded over the years. Many liaisons have been no secret, but his customary discretion, and perhaps an uncustomarily respectful press, have deprived the public of any spicy play-by-play.

Some women to whom he's been linked, like Scarlett Johansson and Gabrielle Union, have both said publicly that they're just friends, while others, unnamed and their virtue undocumented, have been spied entering and exiting the back door of Jeter's bachelor pad at Trump World Tower.

"Derek has girls stay with him at his apartment in New York," a friend—perhaps soon-to-be-ex-friend—dished in 2011, "and then he gets them a car to take them home the next day. Waiting in his car is a gift basket containing signed Jeter memorabilia, usually a signed baseball."

Score one for #2.

"One summer," the friend continued, "he ended up hooking up with a girl he had hooked up with once before, but Jeter seemed to have forgotten about the first time and gave her the same identical parting gift, a gift basket with a signed Derek Jeter baseball."

Oops. E6. ◆

THE JETER PRINCIPLE

ON MIXED MARRIAGES

What if you fell in love with a Red Sox fan—could you marry her?

JETER: I don't think it'd be a question of "Could I?" It'd be a question of "Could she?"

But you could?

JETER: I could probably convert her. But I don't know if her family would allow such a thing.

ABOVE: A week after announcing his retirement at the end of the 2014 season, and 22 years after joining the Yankees organization, Jeter held a standing-room-only press conference.

DEREK JETER'S GUIDE TO SURVIVAL IN NEW YORK CITY

BY JOEL SHERMAN

FEBRUARY 12, 2014

Derek Jeter is the star we knew so well—and not at all. He hid in plain sight. He talked often and said little. He was private even while being public. This has made Jeter both frustrating and admirable for a journalist. He never let you in: frustrating. He never let you in: admirable.

Jeter has a code he has followed right to the end, announcing his retirement on his terms, in as close to a leak-proof way as is possible in 2014—on his Facebook page. Only his die-before-they-would-betray-him confidants were aware of what he was readying to do. He was never going to put his reputation, status, or off-field endeavors—commercial and charitable—in peril by saying the wrong thing at the wrong time.

I have interviewed Jeter on hundreds, probably thousands, of occasions over the past two decades. The first one-on-one was over lunch in a Bennigan's in Tampa. He was a teenager, but he already had all the traits in place that would be there in his 20s and 30s. He made eye contact. He was polite. Whether natural or learned, his answers were distilled of controversy.

I wanted to know more about him and never felt I truly got in. He was warmly cold—receptive to the questions, guarded in the answers. In the end, I knew what everyone knew. He loved two items above all else: his family and being the Yankees' shortstop.

Everything else you merely glimpsed or saw through others. It allowed him to maintain a pristine image, shun scandal, rise above an age when so much is spilled into the public trough for dissection and ridicule. Fans loved him for what they thought they knew.

In two decades, Jeter has gone off the record with me one time. Once. To tell me the name of a player who big-leagued him in the

He was a teenager, but he already had all the traits in place that would be there in his 20s and 30s.

CORE FOUR NO MORE: Jeter said good-bye to Posada in 2012 and Rivera (top) and Pettitte (below) in 2013. Now we'll say good-bye to him.

minors. That was it. He was never going to risk putting his private thoughts or his private life in the hands of others. He couldn't stop you from clicking on a picture of him with Mariah Carey or Minka Kelly, but he wasn't going to explain their status. You could get the entire clubhouse to discuss the temperature in the Jeter–Alex Rodriguez relationship, but not Jeter.

Jeter was so often compared and contrasted with Rodriguez, and he distinguished himself from his frenemy in two vital ways. First, he is discreet. Second, he is simply the most self-confident athlete I have ever covered, which is quite a title because he played side-by-side with Mariano Rivera.

This is where he was most admirable. Everyone cares to some degree what the public or media thinks. But he never betrayed what was important to him to curry a positive spin. He knew some reporters better and longer than others, but did not play favorites. He had a sweet spot for responses—non-controversial, non-condescending—and he stayed in that sweet spot no matter how many off-speed questions were thrown at him year after year.

He would not go out of his way to point out a subtle maneuver on or off the field that could have been missed. You would find out often much later about what he said in a meeting, or when he pulled a player aside, or about an injury that he had played through. When confronted, Jeter would not confirm, not deny, simply sidestep, move along. He didn't need approval from the universe, or from you, just from his family and those who meant the most to him. In an open-book age, he had the fortitude to keep his closed.

So some of what we think we know about Jeter is what we project onto him. The rest is

ABOVE: Back in 2008, Jeter said farewell to the old Yankee Stadium.

there for all to see. He is loyal. Tough. Principled. He loved to play, to compete. He didn't need to *tell* you he loved big moments. He'd rather just provide them.

He has been a great baseball player, one of the outliers who help make a team better by being so consistent in temperament in a day-after-day sport that can grind others down. He makes everyone better because he exports his confidence that he will succeed to his teammates, that the team will prosper, find a way.

He announces his retirement now and gets to control his message again. He doesn't gamble, holding it all season and having the secret trickle out. He doesn't wait for the possibility that he has a poor season because then it might look as if he is being pushed from the game rather than exiting on his own terms.

And he now gets a season-long farewell from a sport that admires him because it senses in him all those qualities he never bragged about, never needed to state publicly to stroke his ego or fan some fame. ◆

THE JETER PRINCIPLE

ON THE MEDIA

Anyway, I was listening to the radio, and they were talking about maybe—

JETER: I don't listen to the radio, so wherever you're going with that question, I don't even want to hear it.

2014

Derek allowed me to stay in the draft as a shortstop, him and Cal Ripken, to not let them say, 'Hey, let's stick this guy at third base.' It allowed me to fulfill my dream and stay at shortstop."—TROY TULOWITZKI, COLORADO ROCKIES SHORTSTOP

THE THINGS HE'LL LEAVE BEHIND

BY MIKE VACCARO

FEBRUARY 13, 2014

Do you want to see the full impact of Derek Jeter's time as a Yankee? Attend a Little League game or an American Legion game or a high school baseball game anywhere in our area once the snow melts and the baseball fields bloom— across the street from Yankee Stadium, outward toward the suburbs of Jersey and Westchester and Connecticut, even in Queens, allegedly enemy turf.

Look at the kids who come to the plate one after the other, and see how alike they all look: right arm up, absently asking for time from the umpire, then both hands on the bat, the right elbow cocked up near the ear, the bat waving like a wand high above their heads—the un-mistakable stance of a Derek Jeter at-bat.

Ask the kids on the team how many of them asked for No. 2. Before Jeter, that was an almost invisible number, not only in baseball but throughout sports. How much? You could argue that before 1995, the most famous ath-lete to wear No. 2 was a horse—that was the number Secretariat wore when he won the '73 Belmont Stakes by 31 lengths.

OPPOSITE: Jeter has signed his name on the game itself. RIGHT: Looking after another great, Phil Rizzuto.

You only hope to be kind of close to him. He's at the top of the mountain and it's a very high mountain to climb. If you get halfway up or three-quarters of the way up, that would be fantastic in anybody's eyes. . . . Just being on the field with him, just being in his presence, is all I could ever ask."—IAN DESMOND, WASHINGTON NATIONALS SHORTSTOP

Now kids bargain and barter and beg for 2.

This is what Jeter's impact has been. You want to define his career by the numbers—by the five world championships, by the 3,316 hits, by the 13 All-Star appearances and the five Gold Gloves, by the eight times he finished in the top 10 of MVP voting and the .312 lifetime average? You can do that.

If you prefer a collection of forever snapshots—the "Flip Play" in Oakland that saved Game 3 of the 2001 ALDS; the home runs that led off Game 4 of the 2000 Subway Series and ended Game 4 of the '01 World Series (and, sure, the one that was redirected by Jeffrey Maier in the '96 ALCS); the fact that his 3,000th hit was also a home run; the hundreds of times he pulled off his jump throw to first from deep in the shortstop hole, a move

It's hard to walk across this public stage for 20 years and emerge unscathed. Yet Jeter did.

318FT

THE JETER PRINCIPLE

ON OWNING THE YANKEES

If the Yankees were ever for sale, you'd be interested, I assume?

JETER: They'd have to give me a BIG discount.

've always looked up to Jeter a lot. Everything he does on the field and the way he carries himself off the field, is unbelievable. What I learned from Jeter is that if he goes 0-for-4, he's still the same guy. He plays the game right. We're going to miss him."—HANLEY RAMIREZ, **LOS ANGELES DODGERS SHORTSTOP**

so famous it became a logo—that's perfectly acceptable, too.

But if you want the full impact, just look around. Look at all those amateur ballplayers. Hell, look at the kids (and the grown-up kids) playing softball and stickball and Wiffle ball in your neighborhood who also channel Jeter.

Every now and again, we get an athlete who not only thrills us on the field, but carries us beyond. Once upon a time, there were millions of New York kids who yearned to be cool like Clyde Frazier, who wanted to walk the walk like Joe Willie Namath, who mimicked every move the Oklahoma Kid, Mickey Mantle, made.

They weren't just stars, they were icons.

Jeter may well be the last of them, too. We know too much about stars now. There is so little mystery attached to them, partly because of our 24/7 world, partly because their failings are inescapable. It's hard to walk across this public stage for 20 years and emerge unscathed.

Yet Jeter did. Even as New York's most eligible bachelor for two decades, he was a relatively rare visitor to Page Six. You never saw a parent discourage their son or daughter from adopting Jeter as their hero, because they believed, absolutely, that he would never disappoint.

And remarkably—incredibly—he never did. ◆

This is what I admire most about Derek Jeter: Consistency. He is the same guy on and off the field. . . . He is the gold standard to follow . . . because you know with Derek no matter what happens today, he is coming to the park to do anything and everything it takes to win a game tomorrow. He has never played a meaningless game." —ALEX RODRIGUEZ

TAKE MY CAREER. PLEASE.

BY MIKE VACCARO

APRIL 7, 2014

He clings to the notion that everything is business as usual, same as it was in 1996 and '99, same as 2004 and '07 and '11. It's understandable. You can't play baseball in dusty rooms, with the emotions of moments overwhelming you, not if you want this to be more than a cheesy thanks-for-the-memories victory lap.

"It's hard," Derek Jeter said, "to be reflective this early."

But Jeter *has* brought something different to the party this year, and in some ways it wouldn't have been as surprising if he'd decided to play the whole season left-handed. He doesn't even have to remind us day to day (as civic law demands) how much fun he's having; it's *obvious* how much fun he's having.

Just look at him.

But even more: just listen to him.

For years, teammates have tried to explain Jeter, and normally what you get are the usual bouquets and sobriquets: he's the captain, he's the forerunner, he's the clubhouse leader for intangibles, he works harder, smarter, longer than anyone, he's a great teammate. During spring training, briefly, Andy Pettitte added something else.

"Jete," he said, "is a very funny guy."

That was something you figured you'd have to file away under the heading of "Things That Might Be True, but We'll Never Know for Sure." It's possible that Al Pacino is really good at telling knock-knock jokes. It's possible that Springsteen has the 10 best lines from *The Sting* memorized, and he recites them at parties.

Might be true.

We'll never know for sure.

Yet as spring training grinded on, and as the season began, if you spent enough time around Jeter you started to hear something different. He has always been accommodating. He has always been accountable. He has always made a habit of standing in front of his locker, even after torturous losses, even last year, when he had to keep finding different ways to tell us how much his foot hurt.

This year has been different, though. There are more pauses, so he can come up with better responses. There are more smiles, more

ABOVE LEFT TO RIGHT: Yukking it up with the press, Tim Raines and the late Don Zimmer.

self-deprecation. And, yes: more laughter. Son of a gun. Jeter really *is* a funny guy.

There were a few persistent questions after this 4-2 home-opening win for the Yankees, for instance, regarding the scorching line drive he hit leading off the fifth, a ball he thought was a homer at first, then a foul ball, and then, as it smacked off the "318" sign in left, ricocheted toward left-fielder David Lough, a ball that caused a priceless look to hijack his face: *I'd better scoot.*

"I picked up the speed when I needed it, to show that my legs were good," he said, chuckling, instantly muting all follow-up questions that might have included the words "Robinson" and "Cano." "It was like an audition."

Someone asked if he was a little embarrassed, a guy known for hustling out routine 4-3 grounders needing a little giddyup to reach second.

"Well, I was safe," he said. "It would've been more embarrassing if I was out."

More smiles. More laughter. More questions: did he find it odd—even a little awkward—that when he grounded into a run-scoring double-play in the third he was still given a sizable ovation from fans who have been known to boo the Cotton-Eye Joe guy?

"Maybe they cheered for me hustling," he said, deadest deadpan ever.

And what of the Moment, capital M, of which there will be so many this year? It was his final home opener, after all. Was there anything—bat, ball, lineup card, sanitary hose, any souvenir at all—that he planned to take with him, to commemorate the last time he'd ever line up along the first-base line in Yankee Stadium in April?

Another halt. In the past, these pauses would allow him to calculate the most vanilla, most diplomatic, least edgy response to any given question. Now we get something else. Now we get this:

"Nah," he said. "Steiner takes everything."

So nobody is free from Jeter's Rickles-ian rapier, not the fans, not his teammates, not Charlie Steiner, memorabilia hoarder. He keeps this up, it won't only be his devotees who'll clamor in October like political acolytes shouting "One more year!" Nope. The folks in the press box with notebooks needing to be filled will be yelling even louder for Shecky Jeter. ◆

EPILOGUE:
OF COURSE HE WAS
BY MIKE VACCARO

This was the spring of 2006. Across the next few months, Derek Jeter would put together what may well have been the finest season of his career. He would collect 214 hits, and he would hit .343, and he would drive in ninety-seven runs, and he would be successful on thirty-four of his thirty-nine steal attempts, a career high. He would win a third straight Gold Glove, and finish second in the voting for the American League's Most Valuable Player, the highest he would ever place.

In August of that year his manager, Joe Torre, would say this about Derek Jeter, two months past his 32nd birthday: "I look at him and I honestly think he might be able to play longer, and better, than anyone I've ever seen because he not only works so hard but he *enjoys* working so hard."

He was, in short, at the peak of his powers.

He was, most likely, among the most famous citizens in the United States, probably among the most admired, certainly among the most idolized.

That's what I wanted to talk to him about early one morning at Legends Field in Tampa. Jeter wasn't on the list of Yankees traveling to Bradenton that morning to play the Pirates. He'd arrived early, gotten his work in, had a

charity function later in the day he didn't want anyone to know about.

"Hey, buddy," he said.

That was the Jeter salutation for the length of his career, for anyone who didn't share the pinstriped vestments. If he was mad at you for whatever reason—a tough question, a tougher article, whatever—maybe he'd suspend the "buddy" part, but never for very long. Even if he knew your name—and he made a point of knowing just about everyone's name—he rarely used it.

I started to ask my battery of questions, but he stopped me.

"You feeling okay?"

I'd had some health issues a few months earlier, been out of the newspaper for a few

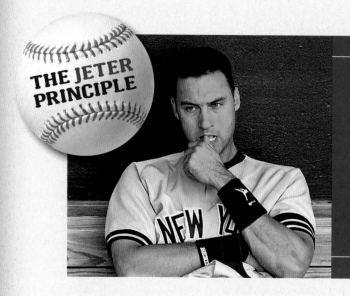

THE JETER PRINCIPLE

On What You Don't Know About Him

Would you want Denzel Washington to play you in *The Derek Jeter Story*?

JETER: Him or Will Smith.

Why Will Smith?

JETER: He's kind of goofy. I'm goofy. You guys don't know. But I got a funny side.

weeks. This was the first time an athlete I covered had asked.

"I'm good," I said. "I'm tougher than I look."

"Okay. What's on your mind?"

It was unremarkable, honestly, and that's what I have always found most remarkable. He wasn't trying to curry favor with a columnist. He wasn't putting on a show for the players at neighboring lockers, or for visiting journalists who might witness this concern. This was simply who Jeter was, and what he was: raised to treat others with respect, expected to understand without comment what regular people do in regular-people situations. Understanding by instinct the proper way to be, the perfect way to behave, the ideal way to conduct himself.

Making it look as natural as breathing.

"People ask me what makes Derek a good captain," says Joe Girardi, who played alongside Jeter from 1996 through 1999, and who managed him for the final seven years of his career. "Mostly, you think of a captain, and a good one, they all have certain qualities you touch on: 'He's a *leader*, and he *leads from the*

front.' Or 'his teammates *respect* him,' or 'they *admire* him,' or 'they'll *follow him into the fire.*' And, look, all of that applies to Derek, too.

"But there's also this: If you didn't know he was the captain, you'd know he was the captain. It's how he treats kids up from the minors. It's how he greets rivals who've been traded here, or signed here. It's how he finds a player who's been released, or traded, or sent down, talks to them, offers them counsel. Almost all of that not only absent from your eyes, but my eyes, too."

It was here Girardi smiled.

"And here's the thing: he was doing that long before Mr. Steinbrenner gave him the title. And that's what makes it different. Some guys are appointed captain. Some guys act the part. I think it's a rare breed of cat who just *is* a captain, a leader, a positive force, however you want to describe it."

That seems apt, too. Ask Jeter what makes a good captain. He'll shake his head. He'll smile. If the mood strikes him, he'll make a self-deprecating joke—as he's gotten older, he's gotten a lot better at sharing a sharp, observational sense of humor with the public. But he won't give you much about his secrets of leadership. Because there are none. This is who he is. This is who he would have been whether he was a baseball player, a firefighter, or a business executive.

"People always wonder more about how or why I do a certain thing than I do," Jeter said not long ago. "I just do what I always do. I do what I've been raised to do, and trained to do."

Maybe that's why so many big moments seemed to find Jeter through the years, and why he took them all in stride. And it wasn't always the obvious play. Some of them were. More often, though, what we got was The Flip play, which was entirely the product of instinct and good habits—two qualities we all want in our children, but don't necessarily expect in a lavishly compensated athletic superstar. Or the near-suicidal dive into the stands against the Red Sox, leaving him bloodied, bruised, battered, and in the hospital . . . and all he cared to talk about, even as he felt like walking death the next few days, was that he made the catch, that the Yankees won.

"With most guys, they're in the right place at the right time, you shake your head at how lucky they are," says Jason Giambi, who was on the other side of The Flip play and later shared a clubhouse with Jeter as a Yankee for seven years. "But Derek was always in the right place. Because . . . because of course he was."

Because of course he was. ◆

PHOTOGRAPHIC CREDITS

Page vii – Nury Hernandez

Page xi – Nury Hernandez

Page xii – *Kalamazoo Gazette*/Landov

Page 8 – AP/Mark Lennihan

Page 11 – Susan May Tell

Page 20 – AP/Mark Lennihan

Page 22 – Bolivar Arellano

Page 29 – W.A. Funches Jr.

Page 30 – Nury Hernandez

Page 31—Francis Specker

Page 42 – Francis Specker

Page 54 – Nury Hernandez

Page 56 – Nury Hernandez

Page 78 (left two photos) – Susan May Tell

Page 83 – Chad Rachman

Page 91 (left photo) Nury Hernandez

Cooperstown photographs are public domain.

All other photographs are by Charles Wenzelberg.

ACKNOWLEDGMENTS

This book was put together by two squads of terrific team players, beginning with the *New York Post*'s Publisher Jesse Angelo, Executive Sports Editor Christopher Shaw, Managing Editor David Boyle, Photo Imaging Editor Dave Johnston, Chief Photographer Charles Wenzelberg, Director of Editorial Research Laura Harris, and all the sportswriters and photographers whose work appears in these pages.

For HarperCollins, Executive Editor David Hirshey, Art Director Leah Carlson-Stanisic, Designer Renato Stanisic, Executive Managing Editor Dori Carlson, Associate Publisher Amy Baker, and editorial assistant Sydney Pierce all worked their usual magic. Thank you, everyone!

R. D. Rosen
Editor

ABOUT THE *NEW YORK POST*

ABOUT THE EDITOR

The *New York Post* chronicles the triumphs and tragedies of New York City through a bold, irreverent, and edgy tabloid design that readers know and love. Founded in 1801 as the *New-York Evening Post*, it is the nation's oldest continuously published daily newspaper.

R. D. Rosen has edited numerous sports books, including *The World Cup Companion* and *Kiss 'Em Goodbye: An ESPN Treasury of Failed, Forgotten, and Departed Teams*, and is the author of a series of mystery novels featuring former major league baseball player Harvey Blissberg. His latest nonfiction book is *Such Good Girls: The Journey of the Holocaust's Hidden Child Survivors*.